Stoic Kids

Big Feelings Edition

Stoic Kids

Big Feelings Edition

44 Stories to Help Kids Handle Anger, Anxiety, and Self-Control

Rodolfo Costa

Title*: Stoic Kids: Big Feelings Edition – 44 Stories to Help Kids Handle Anger, Anxiety, and Self-Control*
ISBN: 979-8-9936270-1-4
Imprint: RC Independently Published

Disclaimer

The content in *Stoic Kids: Big Feelings Edition – 44 Stories to Help Kids Handle Anger, Anxiety, and Self-Control* is intended for educational, inspirational, and entertainment purposes only. While the lessons are rooted in ancient Stoic philosophy and aim to encourage emotional growth and positive values in children, this book is not a substitute for professional psychological, medical, educational, or legal advice.

Parents, educators, and caregivers are encouraged to use discretion and consider individual circumstances when reading or discussing the material with children. The author and publisher assume no responsibility or liability for any loss, injury, or consequence resulting from the use of the ideas or activities described in this book.

Any references to third-party websites, products, or resources are provided for convenience and do not imply endorsement. The author and publisher are not responsible for the content, availability, or accuracy of any external resources mentioned.

By reading and using this book, you agree that all interpretations and decisions based on its content are your own responsibility.

Dedication

For the kids — the future philosophers, the steady hearts, and the brave souls — who are learning that their greatest strength is not in their muscles, but in their minds. This book is for your journey.

Table of Contents

A Note to Grown-Ups. xiii

Welcome, Young Reader!. xv

Part 1: The Fire (Managing Anger & Frustration) 1

1. The Broken Toy (Accepting What We Can't Change) . . . 3
2. The Unfair Referee (Focusing on Our Own Effort). 7
3. The Long Wait (Finding Patience in the Queue). 11
4. The Name-Caller (Understanding That Words Only Hurt If We Let Them) 15
5. The Lego Tower Disaster (Starting Over With a Calm Mind). 19
6. The "It's Not Fair" Cake (Practicing Justice over Greed) . . . 23
7. The Red-Face Monster (Using the "Stoic Pause" to Cool Down) 27
8. The Broken Promise (Controlling Our Reaction to Others' Mistakes) 31
9. The Video Game Glitch (Frustration as a Chance to Practice "The Gap") 35
10. The Loud Neighbor (Choosing Peace in a Noisy World). 39

Part 2: The Storm (Facing Anxiety & Worry) 43

11. The Big Test (Worrying About the Grade vs the Study) 45
12. The Scary Shadow (Stripping Things of Their "Scary" Masks) 49
13. The "What If" Game (Replacing "What If It Goes Wrong?") 53
14. The New Neighborhood (Seeing Change as Natural Part of Life) 57
15. The Stormy Night (Nature Follows Its Own Rules) 61
16. The Dentist's Chair (Pain Is Temporary; Our Courage Is Permanent) 65
17. The Messy Bedroom (Breaking Big Worries into Small Manageable Pieces) 69
18. The Invisible Audience (Realizing Others Aren't Judging Us) 73
19. The Tomorrow-Worrier (Staying in the Present Moment) 77
20. The Map That Changed (Being Flexible When Plans Fall Through) 81

Part 3: The Mountain (Building Confidence & Courage). . . . 85

21. The First Day of School (Courage Isn't the Absence of Fear) 87

22. The Talent Show (Performing for Yourself, Not the Crowd). 90

23. Learning to Ride (Falling Is Just Data for Your Next Try). 94

24. The "I Can't" Wall (Turning Obstacles Into The Way Forward). 98

25. The Question in Class (The Bravery of Being Curious). 102

26. The Secret Skill (Confidence Comes from Doing the Work) 106

27. Standing Up for Sam (The Courage to Be Just When It's Hard) 110

28. The Solo Hike (Finding Strength in Being Alone With Your Thoughts) 114

29. The Mistake on Stage (Owning Your Errors with a Stoic Smile) 118

30. The Giant Leap (Doing the Right Thing Because It Is Right). 122

Part 4: The Anchor (Finding Gratitude & Contentment) . . . 127

31. The Rain on the Picnic Day (Finding the Fun in the Puddles) 129

32. The Lost Favorite Shirt (Nothing Is Truly Ours; It's Only "On Loan") 133

33. The Power of "Enough" (Gratitude for What We Already Have). 137

34. The Hand-Me-Down Bike (Finding Value in Use, Not "Newness") 141

35. The Quiet Saturday (Contentment, Without Needing a Screen). 145

36. The View from Above (Realizing How Small Our "Big" Problems Really Are) 149

37. The Garden of Patience (Waiting for Things to Grow in Their Own Time) 153

38. The Shared Treat (Joy of Being a "Social Being"). 157

39. The Old Dog's Lesson (Living Fully in the "Now") 161

40. The Sunset Reflection (Ending the Day with a Grateful Heart). 165

Part 5: The Compass (Living Your Stoic Superpowers) 169

41. The Morning Mental Armor (Setting Your Intention Before the Day Starts) 171

42. The Evening Review (The Coach's Secret). 175

43. The Stoic Friend (The Lighthouse in the Storm) 179

44. The Never-Ending Journey (Stoicism Is a Practice, not a destination) 183

The Epilogue 187

Request for a Review 189

About the Author 191

A Note to Grown-Ups

Dear Parent, Teacher, or Caregiver,

Welcome to Stoic Kids: Big Feelings Edition — a collection of 44 story-based chapters designed to help children build emotional resilience, develop strong character, and learn how to navigate the big feelings that come with growing up. If you enjoyed *Stoic Kids: 44 Stories That Teach Calm, Courage, and Character*, this Big Feelings Edition dives deeper into the moments when emotions feel especially big and hard to manage.

Stoicism is an ancient philosophy practiced by thinkers like Marcus Aurelius, Epictetus, and Seneca. At its heart, it is beautifully simple: we can't always control what happens to us, but we can control how we respond. This book focuses specifically on the moments when those responses are hardest — when anger, anxiety, frustration, or fear feel overwhelming.

These stories introduce Stoic ideas in a gentle, age-appropriate way through short chapters, relatable characters, and practical reflection questions. Each chapter can stand alone or be explored as part of a longer journey. The five themed sections — The Fire (Anger), The Storm (Anxiety), The Mountain (Confidence & Courage), The Anchor (Gratitude & Contentment), and The Compass (Everyday Practice) — help you guide children through the specific emotional challenges they face every day.

Whether you're reading together at bedtime, using it in a classroom, or encouraging quiet self-reflection, this book is meant to be both a conversation starter and a long-term companion for young captains learning to steer their own ships through any weather.

Thank you for sharing this journey with the young person in your life.

With warm regards,

Rodolfo

Welcome, Young Reader!

Hello, kids!

You're about to explore a book filled with big ideas, told through simple stories that are fun, meaningful, and easy to understand.

This book is all about learning to be strong on the inside. That means:

- Staying calm when the Fire of frustration starts to burn.
- Being kind, even when it's hard.
- Facing your fears like a climber on a high Mountain.
- Choosing what's right, even when no one is looking.

That's what Stoicism is all about. It's not about being a robot or pretending everything is okay. It's about learning to be the Captain of your own ship. Even when the sea gets Stormy, you have the power to stay steady, patient, and wise.

In these pages, you'll meet characters just like you. They learn how to use their Stoic Superpowers to handle anger, worry, bravery, self-control, and gratitude. At the end of each story, there are questions just for you, to help you grow into the strong, kind person you want to be.

So take a deep Stoic breath, turn the page, and get ready. Your journey to becoming a wise and steady Captain starts right here.

Let's go!

Part 1: The Fire (Managing Anger & Frustration)

Building the "Stoic Gap" between what happens and how you react.

Anger is like a spark in a dry forest. If you catch it early, you can blow it out with a single breath. But if you let it grow, it becomes a fire that burns everything in its path. In this section, you'll practice finding the **Stoic Gap**—that tiny, powerful moment between something happening (the spark) and what you choose to do next (the fire).

Every story shows a different kind of "fire": broken things, unfair calls, long waits, mean words, accidents, jealousy, sudden noise, and even glitchy screens. In each one, your superpower is the same: learning to be the boss of your reaction.

Chapter 1

The Broken Toy
(Accepting What We Can't Change)

Leo was an inventor. His workshop wasn't a fancy garage; it was the corner of the living room rug. His greatest invention yet was "The Star-Cruiser," a spaceship made of over a thousand tiny plastic bricks that had taken him three whole Saturdays to build.

He was just about to add the final laser cannon when his younger brother, Sam, zoomed through the room in a superhero cape. Sam wasn't looking. His cape caught the edge of Leo's workspace.

With a sickening crash, the Star-Cruiser hit the hardwood floor. Bricks flew in every direction. Three Saturdays of work disappeared in three seconds.

Heat rushed from Leo's stomach into his chest. His face burned. His hands balled into fists. He wanted to yell. He wanted to grab Sam's favorite toy and throw it.

But then, he remembered something his teacher had said about the **Stoic Gap**—the tiny pause between what happens and what you do next.

Pause, Leo thought, just for three breaths.

He stood perfectly still. Sam was frozen too, staring at the mess with wide, scared eyes.

"I'm sorry, Leo! It was an accident!" Sam whispered.

First breath. The pieces on the floor didn't jump back together.

Second breath. The ship was still broken.

Third breath. Sam was still there, looking guilty and a little bit scared.

In that gap, Leo noticed something important. The spaceship was already broken; that part was over. No amount of yelling could rewind time or lift the bricks off the floor. The only thing still in his control was what happened between him and Sam.

If I scream, I lose my brother and the ship, Leo realized. *If I stay calm, I still lose the ship… but I keep my brother.*

He took one more deep breath. The fire in his chest cooled from an explosion to a warm glow.

"It's okay, Sam," Leo said, his voice a little shaky but calm. "It was an accident… help me find the pieces? We might have to build an even better version now."

Sam's shoulders dropped with relief. "I'll find every single one!" he said, diving to the floor.

As they searched under the couch and between the rug fibers, Leo noticed how different the room felt from just a minute before. The ship was still gone, but there was no shouting, no slammed doors, no tears—just two brothers cleaning up together.

Leo couldn't control Sam's cape or gravity. But he could control what came out of his mouth and what he did next—and that felt stronger than any spaceship.

💭 What the Stoics Would Say

Marcus Aurelius once wrote:

"You have power over your mind—not outside events. Realize this, and you will find strength."

Leo's ship was lost, but his power to choose his next move was still there. That quiet decision— to protect his relationship with his brother instead of his anger—is exactly the kind of strength Marcus meant.

🧠 Stoic Superpower

- **The Three-Breath Rule:** When you feel the Fire of anger, take three slow breaths before you speak or move. That tiny pause is your Stoic Gap.
- **Fix the Mess, Not the Person:** Ask, "Will yelling fix this?" If the answer is no, save your energy for cleaning up and calming down, not attacking someone's feelings.

- **The Power of "Already":** Tell yourself, "This has already happened." You can't change the last three seconds, but you completely own the next three.

🔍 Your Turn to Reflect

- Think of a time someone accidentally broke something of yours or messed up your work. How did your body feel in that moment?
- If you could go back, where would you put your Three-Breath Rule? What might you do differently after the pause?
- Why do you think Leo felt stronger when he chose the relationship instead of getting angry?

Chapter 2

The Unfair Referee (Focusing on Our Own Effort)

The gym was loud with squeaking sneakers and cheering parents. It was the final minute of the regional basketball playoffs, and Sofia's team, the Blue Jays, was down by one point.

Sofia dribbled down the court, heart pounding like a drum. She saw an opening, leaned in for a layup, and—THWACK!—an opposing player bumped her arm. The ball flew out of bounds.

Sofia looked at the referee, waiting for the whistle.

It never came.

"Out of bounds! Red ball!" the referee shouted, pointing the other way.

Sofia froze. "But he hit my arm! That's a foul!" she cried.

The referee didn't even look at her. "Play on," he said.

The Fire hit Sofia instantly. It wasn't just heat; it was that sharp, unfair feeling that makes your eyes sting. Because of that missed call, the other team ran down the court and scored again. The buzzer blared. The game was over.

The Blue Jays had lost.

As the teams lined up to shake hands, Sofia felt rooted to the floor. She didn't want to shake anyone's hand—especially not the referee's. She wanted to refuse, to complain, to sit on the bench and think about how unfair the world was.

Her coach, Coach Miller, saw her face. He walked over and put a hand on her shoulder.

"I know," he said quietly. "He missed the call. It was unfair."

"We lost because of him!" Sofia snapped, her voice trembling.

Coach Miller knelt so he was eye-level with her.

"Sofia, think like a Stoic for a second. Can you go back in time and blow that whistle for him?"

"No," she muttered.

"Can you control what that referee thinks or sees?"

"...No."

"Then why hand him your peace of mind?" Coach Miller asked gently. "The scoreboard, the whistle, the bounce of the ball... those don't belong to us. But your effort? That belongs to you. You played the best defense of the season in those last five minutes. That's your victory. Don't give that away to one bad call."

Sofia looked up at the scoreboard, then back at her teammates. She realized that as long as she stared at the referee, she couldn't see what she'd done well. Staying angry was like letting the whistle keep blowing inside her chest.

She took a slow breath, then another. The heavy feeling loosened, just a little.

Maybe I didn't win the game, she thought, but I did win my part of it.

Sofia walked over and shook the referee's hand. It still felt unfair, but it didn't feel like it owned her anymore. Then she turned to her teammates and pulled them into a hug.

They had lost the game on the wall, but she had won something bigger: she had stopped one bad call from deciding whether she could be proud of herself.

💭 What the Stoics Would Say

Epictetus once talked about an archer.

The archer can choose a good bow, aim carefully, and let the arrow fly with full effort. But once the arrow is in the air, a gust of wind can still push it off course. The result doesn't fully belong to the archer; the aiming does.

In Sofia's game, the referee was like that wind. She couldn't control his whistle, but she could control how carefully she "aimed" her effort—and how she judged herself afterward.

🧠 Stoic Superpower

- **Internal Scoreboard:** Instead of only checking the points on the wall, ask, "Did I give my best effort? Was I a good teammate?" That's the score you control.
- **Accepting the "Wind":** When something unfair happens, tell yourself. "This is the wind. I can't stop it, but I can keep my balance."
- **The Handshake Rule:** Show your strength by being respectful—even when you feel wronged. It proves that your character, not the referee, is in charge of you.

🔍 Your Turn to Reflect

- Have you ever felt like a teacher, coach, or parent made an unfair decision? What were you focused on most: the result or your effort?
- How would it change your feelings if you judged yourself by your Internal Scoreboard instead of the final outcome?
- How does it feel to know that no one—not even a referee—can erase the hard work you put in?

Chapter 3

The Long Wait (Finding Patience in the Queue)

It was the hottest Saturday of the year, and Chloe was standing in the longest line she had ever seen. At the front was "The Frosty Falcon," a brand-new ice cream truck that served "Galaxy Sundaes" with glowing sprinkles. Chloe had been thinking about that sundae all week.

But as the sun beat down on the sidewalk, the line didn't seem to move at all.

Chloe shifted from one foot to the other. She checked her watch. Twelve minutes had passed, and they had only moved three steps.

The Fire started to flicker in her chest. It wasn't the huge blast of anger that comes when something breaks; it was a fidgety, itchy kind of frustration. She wanted to huff. She wanted to complain loudly so everyone would know how annoyed she was.

A boy behind her kicked the dirt and whined to his mom, "How much longer? This is taking forever!"

Chloe felt like joining him. It's not fair, she thought. I'm wasting my whole Saturday standing on a hot sidewalk.

Then she remembered the Stoic Gap her book talked about.

She closed her eyes for a second and looked for that tiny space between the slow line and her itchy feelings. Can I make the line move faster? She asked herself. No. Can I make the sun cooler? No.

If I can't change the line, Chloe thought, what *can* I change?

She realized she was spending her time being miserable—like paying for a toy she didn't even want. A Stoic knows time is the most precious thing we have. Did she really want to spend hers being an Impatience Monster?

Chloe decided to play a new game called **The Observation Station**. Instead of staring at the back of the person's head in front of her, she started looking for things she usually ignored.

She spotted a trail of ants carrying crumbs across the pavement—they looked like a tiny, busy army. She noticed the way the sunlight made wiggly patterns on the brick wall. She counted how many different shoe colors she could see in line. She even started imagining what kind of Galaxy Sundae those ants would invent if they owned the ice cream truck.

Her mind felt less itchy. The line was still slow, but the time didn't feel as heavy.

"Next, please!"

Chloe blinked. She was at the front of the line. She hadn't even noticed the last ten minutes go by. The boy behind her was still red-faced and grumpy, but Chloe felt calm and refreshed.

As she took her first bite of the glowing sundae, she realized the wait hadn't been wasted at all. She had used the Stoic Gap to turn a boring sidewalk into a laboratory for her imagination. The ice cream tasted sweet, but being the boss of her own patience tasted even better.

💭 What the Stoics Would Say

Seneca once said:

"He who is brave is free."

He meant that real bravery isn't just about big, dramatic moments, like fighting dragons or running into danger. Seneca meant that being brave also means staying calm when you have to wait, when things feel boring, or when you don't get what you want right away.

🧠 Stoic Superpower

- **The Observation Station:** When you're stuck waiting, look for three tiny things you've never noticed before. It turns "boring time" into "discovery time."
- **Don't Spend Your Time on Anger:** Time is like money. If you spend it being angry while you wait, you lose both your time and your peace. Spend it on something that makes you curious or happy instead.

- **The "How Much Longer?" Flip:** Whenever you want to ask, "How much longer?", switch it to, "What can I do with the *now*?"

🔍 Your Turn to Reflect

- Where is the hardest place for you to wait—at the doctor's office, in a car ride, or in line at school?
- When Chloe saw the boy behind her complaining, did his complaining make the line move faster? What did it actually change?
- What is one imagination game you can play the next time you have to wait for something?

Chapter 4

The Name-Caller (Understanding That Words Only Hurt If We Let Them)

Toby loved recess, but today recess felt like a trap. He sat on the edge of the sandbox, carefully drawing a map of a hidden island with a stick. He was focused and happy.

Suddenly, a shadow fell over his map. It was Marty from a different class, known for having a stinging tongue.

“That looks like a baby’s drawing,” Marty sneered, loud enough for others to hear. “Hey, everyone, look at Toby! He’s playing in the sand like a toddler!”

Toby felt the Fire instantly. It started as a sharp sting in his ears, then a hot rush in his face. He felt small and exposed. He wanted to snap back with something meaner. He wanted to tell Marty his shoes were ugly or that nobody liked him. His muscles tightened, ready to defend his “honor.”

Then Toby remembered a story his mom had told him about a wise Stoic teacher. He took a slow breath and looked for the Stoic Gap.

In that tiny pause, he looked at the words “baby” and “toddler” in his mind. He imagined them as tiny pebbles being tossed at him.

Are those words true? He asked himself. No. I'm ten years old, and I'm an artist.

If the words aren't true, he thought, they're just sounds. If I don't pick them up, they just fall into the sand.

Toby looked up at Marty. Marty was waiting for a reaction from Toby to get mad, cry, or yell. That was the fuel Marty needed to keep his own Fire burning.

Instead of yelling, Toby did something that surprised everyone, including himself. He looked back down at his map.

"I like my map," Toby said calmly. "But you're allowed to think it's babyish if you want to."

Marty blinked. He looked confused. He was used to people getting angry. When Toby didn't catch the pebble, Marty didn't know what to do next. He huffed, kicked a bit of sand nowhere near the map, and walked away to find someone else who would give him the Fire he wanted.

Toby's heart was still beating a little fast, but the heat in his face was gone. He realized Marty hadn't actually hurt him. Marty had thrown a spark, but Toby had refused to be the dry wood that caught Fire.

He picked up his stick and added a mountain to his hidden island. He felt taller than he had five minutes ago. He realized that the meanest words in the world are like rain on a raincoat—they only soak you if you take the coat off.

💭 What the Stoics Would Say

Marcus Aurelius once wrote:

"Choose not to be harmed—and you won't feel harmed. Don't feel harmed—and you haven't been."

He believed our minds are like a fortress. Someone can shout at the walls all day long, but they can't get inside unless we open the gate. When someone calls you a name, they're making noise. You decide whether that noise becomes a wound or just wind.

🧠 Stoic Superpower

- **The Invisible Shield:** When someone says something mean, imagine a clear, strong shield in front of you. The words hit the shield and drop to the ground. They never touch your skin.

- **The Truth Test:** Ask yourself, "Is what they said a fact?" If a kid calls you a giraffe, do you grow a long neck? If not, it's just an opinion—you don't have to collect other people's opinions.

- **Don't Feed the Fire:** Most name-callers want your anger. When you stay calm, you take away their power and keep your own.

🔍 Your Turn to Reflect

- Can you remember a time someone called you a name or said something mean? What happened inside your body when you heard it?
- Why do you think Marty walked away when Toby stayed calm instead of getting angry?
- If your mind is a fortress, who is the only person who can open the gate to let mean words inside?

Chapter 5

The Lego Tower Disaster (Starting Over With a Calm Mind)

Ben was a Master Builder. For three hours, the only sound in his room was the click-clack of plastic bricks. He was creating the "Sky-High Spire," a tower so tall it reached past his knees and nearly to his desk. It had balconies, a landing pad, and a secret trapdoor. It was his masterpiece.

Just as Ben reached for the last translucent blue piece to crown the top, his Golden Retriever, Bear, came thumping into the room. Bear was happy to see Ben. His long, fluffy tail wagged like a windshield wiper on high speed.

Whack! Bear's tail caught the middle of the spire. In slow motion, Ben watched his masterpiece tilt, wobble, and then explode into hundreds of tiny pieces across the floor.

The Fire didn't just flicker; it roared. Ben felt a scream building in his throat. He wanted to throw his shoe at the wall. He wanted to tell Bear he was a "bad dog" and banish him from the room forever. It felt like all three hours of his life had been stolen.

Then he remembered the Stoic Gap.

He looked at Bear, now sitting down, head tilted, tail still wagging, but eyes confused. Then he looked at the pile of bricks.

Pause, Ben told himself. *One... Two... Three...*

In that pause, a thought slipped in: *The tower is gone. That's a fact. But am I gone? My builder-brain is still here. That's the part that matters.*

He realized that while the tower was in pieces, the Master Builder inside him was still perfectly fine. The skills he used to build balconies and trapdoors were still in his brain and in his hands. Bear's tail could knock over bricks, but it couldn't knock over Ben's ability to create.

Ben took a deep breath. The heat in his chest started to cool. He reached out and patted Bear's head.

"It's okay, big guy. You didn't mean it."

Ben looked back at the mess on the floor. Instead of seeing only a disaster, he tried to see a **New Beginning**. He noticed a few bricks that had landed together in a cool shape he hadn't thought of before.

"Actually," Ben whispered, "the first tower was a bit wobbly at the base anyway. This time, I'm going to make the foundation twice as wide."

He sat back down on the rug and started sorting pieces into little piles. The frustration was gone, replaced by a quiet, steady focus He wasn't just rebuilding a tower; he was designing **Sky-High Spire 2.0**—stronger, smarter, and better than before.

Plastic bricks could fall apart. A Stoic builder knows his real strength lives in his mind and his effort, and that part doesn't break, no matter how hard a dog wags its tail.

💭 What the Stoics Would Say

Marcus Aurelius taught that obstacles can become helpers. When something blocks your plan—like a tower crashing to the floor—that problem can turn into your next step forward. The disaster isn't just a loss; it's also a lesson that helps you build something better.

🧠 Stoic Superpower

- **The "Builder, Not the Building":** Tell yourself, "I am the builder. The things I make can break, but my skill stays with me."
- **The "Draft 2.0" Trick:** When you have to start over, don't just redo it—upgrade it. Use the accident as information to improve your next version.
- **The Tail-Wag Test:** Ask, "Was this an attack or an accident?" Most disasters aren't trying to hurt you; they just happen. Save your strong reaction for real harm, not wagging tails or clumsy bumps.

🔍 Your Turn to Reflect

- Have you ever worked really hard on a drawing, a game, or a project, only to have it get messed up? How did you react?
- If Ben had spent the next hour yelling at Bear, would the tower have been rebuilt any faster? What else would he have lost besides the tower?
- What is one thing you've had to start over on? How was your second version different from the first?

Chapter 6

The "It's Not Fair" Cake (Practicing Justice over Greed)

Saturday night meant one thing in Zoe's house: Dessert. Zoe and her brother, Jax, sat at the kitchen table, eyes glued to the counter where their dad sliced a fresh chocolate cake. The smell was amazing—rich, sweet, and cocoa-filled. Zoe could almost taste the fudge frosting.

Dad placed two plates on the table. Zoe looked at hers, then at Jax's.

Her heart skipped a beat, but not in a good way. The Fire started to prickle on her skin. Jax's slice was definitely wider. It had a big, swirling chocolate rose on top, while hers had only a small leaf. It wasn't just cake anymore; it was an injustice.

"It's not fair!" Zoe burst out. "Jax's piece is way bigger! And he got the rose!"

Jax pulled his plate closer. "Dad gave it to me! Stop being a baby, Zoe."

"I'm not being a baby! You always get the bigger one!" Zoe's cheeks burned. She wanted to grab his plate or push her own cake off the table. The delicious smell now just made her feel grumpy and cheated.

Then Zoe's eyes landed on her Stoic Superpower reminder on the fridge. She took a deep breath and looked for the Stoic Gap.

In that pause, she looked carefully at her own plate. It was a beautiful, thick slice of chocolate cake—exactly what she'd been wanting all week.

She asked herself a hard question: If Jax weren't sitting here, would I love this cake?

The answer was yes.

Her cake hadn't changed. It was still sweet, still chocolatey, still exactly what she needed. The only thing that had changed was her mind. She was staring at Jax's **More** and ignoring her own **Enough**.

The Fire of envy started to flicker instead of flare. Zoe realized that "fair" doesn't always mean "exactly the same." Sometimes one person gets the rose, and next time the other person might. But a Stoic's happiness doesn't depend on what's on someone else's plate.

Zoe picked up her fork. "You know what? This cake looks delicious," she said quietly.

Jax looked surprised. He loosened his grip on his plate.

"Yeah, it is," he said. "Want half of my frosting rose?"

Zoe smiled. By choosing to be grateful for what she had, she'd turned a fight into a moment of sharing. She realized that being

just doesn't mean counting every crumb; it means being the kind of person who can enjoy their own portion and feel happy when others enjoy theirs, too.

💭 What the Stoics Would Say

The Stoic teacher Musonius Rufus believed that greed can quietly steal our peace. He taught that we shouldn't be greedy or always looking for more than our neighbor:

"It is not the consuming of food but the desire for food that hinders the wise person."

That means wanting more and more can make us unhappy, even when we already have enough. True strength is being able to sit at a table and be satisfied with your portion. When we stop comparing, we stop letting jealousy boss us around and, we become the masters of our own joy.

🧠 Stoic Superpower

- **The Comparison Killer:** When you feel the "It's Not Fair" Fire, look away from the other person's plate and look at your own. Ask, "Is what I have good?"
- **The "Enough" Shield:** Say to yourself, "I have enough." Greed is a fire that never stops burning because it

always wants more. **Enough** is the cool water that puts that Fire out.

- **Celebrate for Others:** Practice feeling happy when someone else gets something good. It's a superpower because your happiness can grow even when you aren't the one getting the rose.

🔍 Your Turn to Reflect

- Can you remember a time you felt someone else got more than you—maybe a bigger gift, more screen time, or a better seat?
- How did focusing on what they had change how you felt about what you had?
- Why is it sometimes harder to be happy for someone else than to be happy for ourselves?

Chapter 7

The Red-Face Monster (Using the "Stoic Pause" to Cool Down)

Oliver loved his **Quiet Zone**. It was a corner of his room filled with his favorite books and a desk where he built model airplanes. It was the one place where he felt totally in control.

But Oliver had a younger sister named Lily. Lily didn't understand the Quiet Zone. To her, it looked like a Play Zone.

One afternoon, Oliver was carefully gluing a tiny propeller onto a vintage biplane. It was delicate work. Suddenly, the door burst open. Lily came charging in, singing at the top of her lungs and shaking a box of bells. She bumped Oliver's elbow and—smear—a long line of sticky glue went right across the cockpit.

Oliver felt it immediately. The Red-Face Monster was waking up.

First, his ears felt hot, like they were being held near a toaster. Then his heart thumped against his ribs. His face turned a deep, bright pink, and his eyebrows scrunched down so low he could barely see. A giant ROAR built up in his throat. He wanted to scream at Lily to get out and never come back.

Just before the roar escaped, Oliver remembered the **Stoic Pause**.

He didn't say a word. He didn't move. He simply closed his eyes and stayed as still as a statue.

Lily stopped singing. She looked at Oliver, waiting for the explosion. She expected yelling and stomping. But Oliver was busy in his Stoic Gap, counting his breaths.

One… two… three… four…

By five, the heat in his ears began to fade. By ten, his heart had slowed down. He realized something important: the Red-Face Monster was just a feeling. It wasn't *him*. If he didn't give the monster his voice or his hands, the monster couldn't do any damage.

Oliver opened his eyes. He looked at the glue smear. It was annoying, but fixable with a damp cloth. He looked at Lily. She looked a little worried now.

"Lily," Oliver said. His voice was quiet and steady. "When you run in here like that, it makes me feel very frustrated because I'm doing a big job. Please go play in the hallway for a bit."

Lily blinked. She looked at the airplane, then back at her brother.

"Okay, Oliver. Sorry." She turned and walked out quietly, closing the door behind her.

Oliver let out a long sigh. A huge wave of relief washed over him. He realized that if he had let the Red-Face Monster speak, there would have been a big fight, Mom would have been upset, and he would still have a glue smear on his plane. Instead, he had used his Stoic Pause to keep the peace.

He picked up the cloth and wiped the glue away. He wasn't just fixing a plane; he was practicing control over himself. That felt better than roaring ever could.

💭 What the Stoics Would Say

The Stoic philosopher Seneca wrote an entire book about anger. He famously said:

"The greatest remedy for anger is delay."

He believed anger is a "short madness"—it makes us do things we regret. If we can just wait, even for a few seconds, the madness passes, and our wisdom comes back. The Stoic Pause is the little bridge that carries us from being mad to being wise.

🧠 Stoic Superpower

- **The Heat Check:** As soon as you feel your ears get hot or your heart beat fast, say to yourself, "The Monster is here." Just noticing it helps you remember that *you* are in charge.
- **The Statue Trick:** When you feel like screaming, try to be a statue for ten seconds. Don't move your hands, your feet, or your tongue. Let the first blast of anger pass.

- **The "Later" Rule:** Tell yourself, "I can be mad in ten minutes if I still want to, but right now I'll stay quiet." Most of the time, ten minutes later, you won't want to be mad anymore.

🔍 Your Turn to Reflect

- Where do you feel anger first—your stomach, your hands, your face, or somewhere else?
- Why do you think it's harder to stay quiet than it is to yell when you're upset?
- Can you think of a time you let the Red-Face Monster talk for you? What happened afterward, and how did you feel about it later?

Chapter 8

The Broken Promise (Controlling Our Reaction to Others' Mistakes)

Ethan had had his backpack ready by the front door since noon. Today was the day. His dad had promised that as soon as he finished work at 4:00, they would go to "The Gravity Zone," the coolest trampoline park in the city. Ethan could already feel the wind in his hair as he practiced mid-air flips on the living room rug.

4:00 came. Then 4:15. Then 4:30.

Finally, Ethan heard the jingle of keys. The door opened, and his dad walked in. But he wasn't wearing his fun shoes. He looked tired, his tie was loose, and he was still talking on his phone. When he hung up, he looked at Ethan's backpack and let out a long, heavy sigh.

"Oh, Ethan. I am so sorry, buddy," Dad said, rubbing his eyes. "The computer system at the office crashed. I have to stay on calls all evening to fix it. We can't go to the trampoline park today."

The Fire hit Ethan like a lightning bolt. It was a hot, stinging anger mixed with a heavy dose of sadness.

"But you promised!" Ethan yelled, his voice cracking. "You said Saturday was our day! You lied!"

He felt the urge to stomp up the stairs and slam his door. He wanted to make his dad feel as bad as he felt. He felt like a victim—like his whole Saturday had been ruined by someone else's mistake.

Then Ethan saw his "Stoic Kids" bookmark poking out of a book on the coffee table. He stopped. He took a long, slow breath and stepped into the Stoic Gap.

In that gap, he really looked at his dad. He noticed the dark circles under his eyes and how his shoulders drooped. He realized his dad didn't *want* to be on work calls; he wanted to be jumping on trampolines, too.

Ethan asked himself: Did Dad break the promise because he's mean, or because life is messy?

The anger started to change. It didn't disappear, but it shrank from a roaring fire into a small, warm spark. Ethan realized he couldn't control the office computers or his dad's schedule. But he was still in charge of how the rest of the night would feel for both of them.

"I'm really disappointed, Dad," Ethan said. He was proud that his voice stayed calm. "I was really looking forward to it."

Dad was glad Ethan was handling it so well.

"I know, Ethan. I'm disappointed too," he said. "What if we order your favorite pizza, and while I'm on my calls, you pick out the movie we'll watch together as soon as I'm done?"

Ethan nodded. He still wished he were at the trampoline park. But he also realized something else: slamming his door wouldn't teleport him to Gravity Zone. It would only make him lonely and make his dad feel worse.

By choosing his reaction—by picking the kinder handle—Ethan kept his Saturday from being a total loss. He was the boss of his own mood, and that was a power no broken promise could take away.

💭 What the Stoics Would Say

Epictetus said that everything in life has two handles:

"Every problem in life has two handles, one of which will bear it, and the other not."

He meant that when someone lets you down, you can grab the situation by the **Anger Handle**—focusing only on how unfair it is—or by the **Compassion Handle**—remembering the other person is struggling too. The Anger Handle is too hot to hold. The Compassion Handle lets you carry the disappointment without burning yourself.

🧠 Stoic Superpower

- **The Two Handles:** When someone makes a mistake, ask, "Which handle am I picking this up by?" Choose the handle that keeps you calm.

- **People Are Not Computers:** Remember that even the best people get tired, forget things, or run into emergencies. Expecting them to be perfect every time is a recipe for constant Fire.
- **The Pivot Play:** When a plan breaks, don't sit in the ruins. Pivot. Ask, "What is the second-best thing I can do right now?" and move toward that instead.

🔍 Your Turn to Reflect

- Can you remember a time a parent or friend broke a promise? How did you react?
- If Ethan had yelled and slammed his door, how would his dad have felt during his work calls? How would Ethan's night have felt?
- Why is it helpful to remember that most people don't break promises on purpose?

Chapter 9

The Video Game Glitch (Frustration as a Chance to Practice "The Gap")

Lucas was in the Zone. He was playing Galaxy Quest and was only moments away from defeating the final boss, a giant robotic squid. His thumbs moved like lightning across the controller. He had been trying to beat this level for three weeks.

"Just one more hit!" Lucas whispered, his eyes wide.

Then the unthinkable happened. The music stuttered. The robotic squid froze in mid-air. The screen turned a dull, frozen grey. A tiny spinning circle appeared in the corner.

Lucas tapped the buttons. Nothing. He shook the controller. Nothing. He waited ten seconds, twenty seconds... then the console beeped and restarted itself. His progress was gone. He was back at the beginning of the level.

The Fire exploded. Lucas felt a surge of heat so strong it made his skin buzz. He wanted to hurl the controller at the TV. He wanted to kick the couch and scream at the top of his lungs. It felt like the game had cheated him on purpose.

As his arm pulled back to throw the controller, Lucas caught a glimpse of his reflection in the dark TV screen. He saw his red face and angry eyes.

The Gap, he thought. Find the Gap.

He lowered his arm. He put the controller down on the coffee table slowly, as if it were made of glass. Then he sat back and closed his eyes.

In that small pause, Lucas asked himself: Is this glitch a monster, or is it just code?

He realized that the computer wasn't trying to be mean; it was just a machine that had made a mistake. The game didn't know who he was. It couldn't care about his feelings. He also realized that while he had lost his Level 50 status in the game, he hadn't lost his Level 50 calm in real life—unless he chose to throw it away.

"The game is a toy," Lucas muttered. "I am a Stoic. I don't let machines choose my mood."

He took five deep, slow breaths. The Fire in his chest didn't vanish instantly, but it stopped growing. It cooled into a small pile of embers. He realized that the three weeks he spent playing hadn't been wasted at all: he'd enjoyed the challenge and gotten much better at the game.

A few minutes later, his dad walked into the room. He expected to find Lucas in the middle of a gamer meltdown. Instead, he saw Lucas sitting quietly, looking at a book.

"Everything okay, Lucas? I heard the console reboot," Dad said.

"It glitched right at the end," Lucas said. He even managed a tiny smile. "I was really mad for a second, but then I realized it was a perfect chance to practice the Gap. I think I won the real-life level today, even if I lost the game level."

Lucas picked up the controller again, but he didn't turn the game back on right away. He felt stronger than any robotic squid because he had defeated the hardest boss of all—his own temper.

💭 What the Stoics Would Say

Seneca warned that it doesn't help to get angry at things that can't think or feel. He taught that we should not let our peace be ruined by objects that cannot mean us harm.

A computer, a game, or a toy can't feel your anger and can't apologize. When you rage at a thing, you hand your power over to something that isn't even alive.

🧠 Stoic Superpower

- **The Screen Saver Breath:** When a screen freezes, you freeze too. Don't move your hands until you've taken three slow breaths. Use the loading circle as a timer for your calm.

- **The Real-Life Level-Up:** Tell yourself, "Winning the game is fun, but winning my self-control is a permanent upgrade." Skills in your character last longer than scores in a game.
- **Code vs. Character:** A glitch is just bad code. Don't let bad code create bad character in you.

🔍 Your Turn to Reflect

- Why does it feel so personal when a computer or a game glitches, even though it isn't alive?
- If Lucas had thrown the controller, would the game have fixed itself? What else might have been broken?
- What is one non-living thing that usually makes you feel the Fire of frustration—a slow computer, a stuck zipper, a lost shoe?

Chapter 10

The Loud Neighbor (Choosing Peace in a Noisy World)

Sienna's favorite place in the whole world was her **Reading Nook**. It was a tiny space between her bed and the window, filled with fluffy pillows and a dim lamp. When she was there, she felt as if she were in another dimension.

She had just reached the most exciting part of her book—where the hero was about to discover the secret cave—when a sound shattered the silence.

THUMP. THUMP. THUMP.

It came from the apartment next door. Then a high-pitched squeal and the sound of someone running. It was the Henderson twins. They were playing Indoor Soccer again.

Sienna tried to ignore it. She pressed her hands over her ears and tried to focus on her page.

CRASH!

Something hit the wall right behind her head.

The Fire flared up instantly. Sienna felt a sharp, jagged frustration in her chest. She wanted to stand up and bang on the wall. She wanted to march over and tell them they were ruining her afternoon. It felt like her peace had been stolen.

Then Sienna glanced at her Stoic Superpower wristband. She closed her eyes and searched for the Stoic Gap.

In that tiny space of quiet inside her mind, Sienna asked herself: Are the Henderson twins trying to ruin my book, or are they just being kids? She realized they weren't her enemies; they were just loud. Then she asked: Can I reach through the wall and make them sit still? No.

Sienna realized she had been treating her peace like a glass vase that someone else could knock off a shelf. But the Stoics taught that peace isn't a vase; it's an **Inner Citadel**—a strong stone fortress inside you. If she stayed inside her fortress, the noise outside couldn't touch her.

Instead of banging on the wall, Sienna tried something different. She decided to **invite the noise in**.

Every time she heard a thump, she imagined it was the sound of drums echoing in her book's secret cave. When something crashed, she pictured rocks tumbling as the hero explored deeper. The noise became background music for her adventure.

By changing how she thought about the sound, the sound lost its power to make her angry. She realized the world would always be noisy—sirens, barking dogs, honking cars, loud neighbors. But a Stoic child carries their own silence inside them, like a secret room no one else can enter.

Ten minutes later, the Henderson twins stopped playing. Sienna didn't even notice. She was already deep inside the secret cave, her mind as calm as a mountain lake in a world full of thumps.

💭 What the Stoics Would Say

Marcus Aurelius wrote about finding peace when the world is busy:

"Nowhere can man find a quieter or more untroubled retreat than in his own soul."

He meant you don't need a silent forest to feel calm. You have a Quiet Nook inside your own heart and mind that you can visit whenever you choose. People can make noise, but they can't force you to be noisy on the inside.

🧠 Stoic Superpower

- **The Inner Volume Knob:** When the world gets loud, imagine you have a volume knob in your mind. Turn the World volume down and your Inner Calm volume up.
- **The Citadel Defense:** Remind yourself, "My peace is a fortress. A loud noise is just a tiny pebble hitting a giant stone wall. It can't break me."
- **Borrow the Noise:** Use the noise around you for something else. If someone is tapping a pencil, imagine

it's a clock or part of a song. Don't fight the sound; let it pass through you.

🔍 Your Turn to Reflect

- What is a sound that usually makes you feel the Fire—a sibling crying, a vacuum cleaner, a loud TV?
- If Sienna had banged on the wall and yelled, would the neighbors have become quieter, or would they probably have yelled back?
- How does it feel to know that your Quiet Place is something you carry with you everywhere you go?

Part 2: The Storm (Facing Anxiety & Worry)

The Captain and the Sea: Steering your ship when you can't control the wind or the waves.

Anxiety can feel like being in a small boat in the middle of a dark, choppy ocean, with "What-If" waves crashing over the sides and howling "Worry" winds pushing you around. The Stoics knew that sailors can't control the weather, the size of the waves, or the direction of the wind—but they can always steer their own ship. In this section, you'll practice stopping the fight with the storm and instead focusing on your sails: what you can do right now, rather than what might happen later. The sea won't magically go quiet, but you'll discover you are the steady Captain of your ship, even when the thunder is loud.

Chapter 11

The Big Test (Worrying About the Grade vs the Study)

The week before the Big Math Test, Maya felt like she had a swarm of bees in her stomach. Every time she looked at her calendar and saw the red circle around "Friday," the buzzing got louder.

"What if I forget everything?" she whispered at night. "What if I'm the only one who fails? What if the questions are in a language I don't even know?"

Maya was so busy worrying about Friday that she could barely focus on her homework on Tuesday. Her mind kept jumping ahead to the storm instead of staying with the work in front of her.

On Wednesday, she saw her grandfather on the porch, calmly reading while a light rain began to fall.

"Grandpa, aren't you worried it's going to pour?" Maya asked.

"I can't stop the rain, Maya," he said. "But I checked the roof this morning, and I have my umbrella right here. The rest is up to the clouds."

"I feel like it's raining inside my head about this math test," Maya said, sitting down.

“Ah,” Grandpa replied, closing his book. “You’re trying to control the clouds. Listen: the grade your teacher puts on that paper on Friday is like the rain. You can’t reach into the future and change it. But do you know what your umbrella is?”

Maya thought. “Studying?”

“Exactly,” Grandpa said. “And your roof is getting a good night’s sleep. When you worry about the grade, you’re a Captain shouting at the wind. When you practice your fractions, you’re a Captain trimming the sails. One makes you tired. The other gets you home.”

That night, whenever a “What if I fail?” thought popped into Maya’s head, she pictured herself on a ship.

That thought is just wind, she told herself. I’m going to focus on my sails.

She opened her textbook and practiced five problems. The bees in her stomach didn’t fly away completely, but they stopped buzzing so loudly. Instead of pacing around her room, she spent her energy on what she could actually change.

Friday came. Maya sat down and opened the test. She didn’t know every answer, but she didn’t panic. She knew she had checked her roof, opened her umbrella, and trimmed her sails as well as she could. The storm had arrived, but she wasn’t just a worried passenger anymore. She was a Stoic Captain—and she was ready.

💭 What the Stoics Would Say

Seneca once said:

"We suffer more often in imagination than in reality."

He meant that most of the things we worry about never actually happen—or they aren't as bad as our minds pretend. When we spend all our time worrying about the future rain, we miss the chance to use the sunny time we have right now to prepare.

🧠 Stoic Superpower

- **The Sails Check:** When you feel worried, ask, "Am I thinking about the wind (the grade and the future), or my sails (my practice and effort right now)?"
- **The Five-Minute Rule:** Instead of worrying for an hour, use five minutes to study, practice, or ask for help. Action is the best way to quiet a What-If thought.
- **Stay on the Boat:** Remind yourself, "Right now, I am safe. The test is in the future." Most worries live in a "later" that hasn't happened yet.

🔍 Your Turn to Reflect

- What is one "Big Test" or event coming up that makes you feel like a storm is brewing?
- What is one thing you can do to get ready for the 'Big Test'?
- What is one thing you cannot control, no matter how much you worry?

Chapter 12

The Scary Shadow (Stripping Things of Their "Scary" Masks)

Clara was a brave Captain during the day. She climbed trees, rode her bike without hands, and wasn't even afraid of the big dog next door. But at night, when the dark rolled in, Clara felt like her ship was sinking.

Right after her parents turned out the light and closed the door, a tall, jagged shape appeared in the corner by the closet. It had long, skinny fingers and a hunched-over back. It didn't move. It just stood there, watching her.

Clara pulled the covers to her nose. Her heart started that fast storm drumming. What if it's a monster? she worried. What if it's a ghost waiting for me to fall asleep? The more she stared at the shadow, the scarier it became. In her mind, it grew teeth and glowing eyes.

One night, the storm in her head was so loud she couldn't take it anymore. She remembered something she'd learned about being a Stoic Captain: Look at the waves for what they really are.

Clara took a deep breath. Instead of hiding under the covers, she sat up. She reached for her "Captain's Log" (her notebook) and a small flashlight. She didn't turn the big light on yet. She wanted to face the shadow.

"Okay," Clara whispered, "let's look at you like a Stoic."

She pointed her flashlight low so the room stayed mostly dark and looked closely at the "long, skinny fingers." Without the scary story in her mind, what were they? She squinted.

They were the sleeves of her green hoodie hanging on a hook.

She looked at the "hunched-over back." What was that? Her backpack, stuffed with library books, sitting on a chair.

Clara began to write a list in her notebook:

- One green hoodie (soft cotton, smells like laundry).
- One blue backpack (canvas, holds three books).
- One wooden chair (brown, squeaky leg).

As she wrote the facts, something amazing happened. The "monster" didn't run away; it just stopped existing. The scary feeling came from the story she had told herself, not from the objects in the corner.

Her storm began to calm. Her anxiety had been like a fog that turned everyday things into ghosts. By using her Fact Check, she cleared the fog and saw the room as it really was.

Clara turned off her flashlight and lay back down. The shadow was still on the wall, but now she just saw a hoodie and a backpack. She realized the dark isn't a monster; it's just the light being turned off. The objects are the same as they are in the daytime.

She closed her eyes, steered her ship into quieter waters, and fell asleep. In the morning, she woke up feeling like the strongest Captain in the world because she had learned to see clearly, even in the dark.

💭 What the Stoics Would Say

Marcus Aurelius had a trick for things that scared or tempted him. He said we should:

"Strip them of the legends with which they are adorned."

He meant we should describe things in plain, simple words. A scary shadow isn't a ghost; it's "cotton and light." A scary test isn't a disaster; it's "ink on paper." When we take away the legend—the story—we take away most of the fear.

🧠 Stoic Superpower

- **The Fact Checker:** When you are scared of something, describe it using only facts. "The dark is just a room with no light." "This is fabric on a hook."
- **Strip the Legend:** Ask yourself, "Am I reacting to what is really happening, or to the story I'm telling myself about it?"

- **The 'What Is It Really?' Game:** Look at something that worries you and describe what it's made of: plastic, paper, fabric, wood. Things made of fabric or paper can't hurt your soul.

🔍 Your Turn to Reflect

- Is there something in your room or at school that looks scary until you look closely? What is it really made of?
- Why do you think writing down the facts about a worry can make the worry feel smaller?
- Next time you feel a storm of worry, how could you strip away the legend and see the simple truth underneath?

Chapter 13

The "What If" Game (Replacing "What If It Goes Wrong?")

Mason had to give a presentation on "The History of Robots" in front of the whole fourth grade on Friday. On the outside, he looked like a normal kid. Inside his head, a game was playing—the "What If" Game—and Mason was losing.

What if I trip on the way to the front of the room? The voice whispered. What if I forget every single word? What if the projector breaks and my pictures disappear? What if everyone laughs at me?

By Thursday night, Mason's storm was so loud he couldn't finish his dinner. He felt like a tiny boat being tossed by giant waves that hadn't even reached the shore.

His older sister, Lauren, noticed him staring at his mashed potatoes. Lauren had been practicing Stoicism for a year.

"Mason," she said, "you're playing the wrong version of the game."

"There's only one version," he sighed. "The one where everything goes wrong."

"Nope," Lauren said, sliding him a piece of paper. "That's the Worry Version. Stoics play the Warrior Version. Every time you think of a scary “What If”, you have to finish the sentence with: ‘Then I will…’”

“What do you mean?” Mason asked.

“Try it,” Lauren said. “Give me your scariest “What If”.”

“What if I forget my words?” Mason whispered.

“Okay,” Lauren nodded. “Now finish it like a Captain. ‘What if you forget your words? Then you will…’”

Mason thought. “Then I will… take a deep breath, look at my note cards, and start the sentence again.”

“Exactly!” Lauren grinned. “Now another one.”

“What if everyone laughs?”

“Then I will… remember their laughter is just a sound. It doesn’t change the facts about robots. I’ll wait for them to stop, smile, and keep going.”

For the first time all week, something shifted in Mason’s chest. The storm didn’t feel like it was drowning him. He realized the “What Ifs” were waves; he couldn’t stop them from appearing, but he could decide exactly how to steer through each one.

He wasn’t as afraid of the wave anymore, because he finally had a plan for the splash.

On Friday morning, Mason stood at the front of the room. His hands were a little shaky, and his voice cracked once. But every time a worry popped up, he answered it instantly.

What if I miss a slide? Then I'll explain the next one.

He wasn't waiting for a perfect speech; he was busy being a prepared Captain. When he finished, he didn't care if it was the best speech in the world. He felt huge inside because he had played the "What If Game" and finally won.

💭 What the Stoics Would Say

Marcus Aurelius had a secret for facing the future. He wrote:

"Never let the future disturb you. You will meet it, if you have to, with the same weapons of reason which today arm you against the present."

He meant you don't need to panic about tomorrow's problems, because the same brain and calm you have today will be with you tomorrow. You already carry the "weapons" you need to handle whatever comes your way.

🧠 Stoic Superpower

- **The "Then I Will" Flip:** Every time a What If worry enters your mind, finish the sentence with a plan. "What if I mess up? Then I will..."

- **The Anchor of the Now:** Remind yourself, "The "What If" is in the future, but I am in the Right Now. In the Right Now, I am safe."
- **Wave Watching:** Imagine your worries as waves passing by your ship. You don't have to jump into every wave; you watch them roll past while you keep your hands on the wheel.

🔍 Your Turn to Reflect

- What is one "What If" that's been buzzing in your head lately?
- Can you finish it Stoic-style: "What if [my worry] happens? Then I will…"?
- Why do you think having a plan makes the scary "What If" feel less powerful?

Chapter 14

The New Neighborhood (Seeing Change as Natural Part of Life)

Ava stood in the middle of her bedroom, but it didn't feel like her bedroom anymore. The walls were bare where her posters used to be. Her bed was just a mattress on the floor. Everything she owned was inside brown cardboard boxes.

"I hate change," Ava whispered to her stuffed owl, Barnaby, perched on a box labeled BOOKS.

In two days, Ava's family was moving to a new city, three hours away. A cold, swirling anxiety stormed in her chest.

What if the kids at the new school are mean? What if I get lost in the new house? What if the new neighborhood doesn't have any good climbing trees?

She felt like she was being dragged away from her favorite shore by a current she couldn't fight.

Her mom walked in with a roll of packing tape. She saw Ava's face and sat on the mattress.

"It feels like we're losing everything, doesn't it?" Mom said softly.

"We are," Ava sniffed. "Everything is changing."

"Ava, look at that big oak tree outside," Mom said. "When we first moved here, it was covered in bright green leaves. Then in the fall, every leaf turned brown and fell. All winter, it looked skeleton-thin and cold. Was the tree losing everything?"

Ava thought. "No. It was getting ready for spring."

"Exactly," Mom said. "The tree doesn't cry when the leaves fall, because it knows change is how the world grows. If the leaves never fell, there'd be no room for new buds.

"Life is like a river," she continued. "It never stays in one place. You can try to swim against the current and get exhausted, or you can be a Captain who realizes that a new shore means new adventures."

Ava looked at the oak tree. She realized she had been treating change like a mistake, but it was actually one of nature's rules, just like seasons.

She picked up a marker and grabbed a box. Instead of just writing CLOTHES, she drew a little sailboat on the side.

I am the Captain, she thought. The current is moving me, but I am the one steering.

She started to think about new "buds" that might grow in her new season. Maybe the new house had a bigger backyard. Maybe her new teacher liked space as much as she did. Maybe there was a new climbing tree she hadn't met yet.

The storm didn't disappear, but the wind started to feel like it was pushing her forward instead of knocking her down. She realized she wasn't losing her old life; she was making room for a new chapter.

💭 What the Stoics Would Say

Marcus Aurelius spent a lot of time thinking about how the world is always shifting. He wrote:

"Nature loves nothing so much as to change what is and to create new things like them."

He believed change is the heartbeat of the world. Without it, there would be no growth, no tomorrow, and no you. When we stop fearing change, we can finally notice and enjoy the new gifts the world is trying to show us.

🧠 Stoic Superpower

- **The "Season" Shift:** When things change, ask, "What season am I in?" Remember that even winter is just a way to get to spring.
- **The River Rule:** Imagine life as a river. You can't stop the water from flowing, so don't waste your energy trying. Focus on steering your boat safely through the new turns.

- **The "New Bud" List:** Write down three things you're curious or excited to discover in the new situation, even if they're small.

🔍 Your Turn to Reflect

- Can you think of a time something changed—a new grade, a new friend, a move?
- Looking back, what was one "new bud" or good thing that came out of that change?
- Why do you think the oak tree doesn't worry when its leaves fall off every year?

Chapter 15

The Stormy Night (Nature Follows Its Own Rules)

Finn lay in bed, staring at the ceiling. Outside, the sky was a bruised purple, and the wind whistled through the cracks in the window. A flash of white light filled the room, followed by a low BOOM that made his bed frame vibrate.

Finn pulled his blanket over his head. His heart beat in a fast, stormy rhythm. What if the wind blows the roof off? He thought. What if the lightning is trying to find me? The storm felt like a giant, angry monster stomping around his house.

His dad walked in carrying a small lantern. He saw the shaking lump under the blankets.

"Hey, Captain," Dad said softly, sitting on the bed. "The sea is looking choppy tonight, isn't it?"

Finn peeked out. "Why is the storm so angry? Why is it making so much noise?"

"The storm isn't angry," Dad said, putting down the lantern. "Think about a clock. Does it tick because it wants to annoy you, or because that's just how its gears work?"

"It's just how it works," Finn whispered.

"Nature is the same," Dad said. "Clouds fill up with electricity, then let it out. Wind moves when the air changes temperature. Thunder is just the sound of air snapping back together. Nature isn't mean or kind. It's just following its own rules. It doesn't have a volume knob, and it doesn't know if we're awake or asleep."

Finn had never thought of it that way. He'd been waiting for the storm to apologize or stop "being mean." But you can't be mad at a cloud for being a cloud.

"So what's the Captain's job during a storm?" Finn asked.

"A Captain doesn't yell at the lightning," Dad said. "A Captain checks the sails. Our 'sails' are the roof over our heads, the locked doors, and your warm blankets. Nature's job is to make thunder and rain. Your job is to stay safe and keep your mind calm. You do your job, and let the clouds do theirs."

Finn took a deep breath. He listened to the next BOOM. This time, instead of hearing a monster, he imagined the gears of the world turning. He pictured the rain giving the trees a drink. The storm was just the world doing its work.

"I'm doing my job now, Dad," Finn said, fluffing his pillow. "I'm the Captain of the Calm."

Dad smiled and blew out the lantern. As the rain drummed on the roof, Finn didn't hide. He listened to the rhythm of the world, safe in his ship, while nature followed its own rules outside the window.

🗣 What the Stoics Would Say

The Stoics believed that nature follows its own rules. We don't control the clouds or the lightning—but we do control whether we listen, stay inside, and keep calm. When you accept, "Tonight is stormy," instead of demanding, "It must be clear," you become like a skilled Captain who works with the weather instead of shouting at the sky.

By trusting nature to do its job and focusing on your own, you turn a scary night into a chance to practice courage, patience, and wisdom.

🧠 Stoic Superpower

- **Nature's Job / My Job:** When you are scared of the weather, tell yourself, "The clouds are doing their job. I am doing mine."
- **The Science Shield:** Learn how things work. When you know thunder is just vibrating air and lightning is electricity, they stop being monsters and turn into facts.
- **The Safe Harbor Checklist:** Remind yourself of what keeps you safe: "I have a roof. I have a bed. I have people who love me." Those are your anchors.

🔍 Your Turn to Reflect

- Is there something in nature that scares you—spiders, the dark, loud wind, big waves?
- How does it change your feelings to know nature isn't trying to scare you; it's just following its rules?
- What can you do the next time a storm comes to "do your job" as a Captain?

Chapter 16

The Dentist's Chair (Pain Is Temporary; Our Courage Is Permanent)

Julian sat in the waiting room, and his storm was at Category 5. The room smelled like mint and soap. Every few seconds, he heard the high-pitched whirrr of a drill behind a heavy wooden door.

To Julian, that sound was like a siren warning of a shipwreck.

"Do we have to stay?" he asked his mom. "My tooth doesn't even hurt that much anymore. Maybe it fixed itself?"

Mom smiled and put down her magazine. "Your mind is trying to steer the ship away from the storm," she said. "But sometimes, the only way to get to the quiet harbor is to sail straight through the rain."

When the nurse called his name, Julian's legs felt like jelly. He climbed into the big reclining chair. The bright light above him felt like a miniature sun. His heart raced; the "What-If" monster whispered. What if it hurts? What if I can't stay still?

Dr. Aris, the dentist, noticed Julian's white-knuckled grip on the armrests.

"Julian," he said kindly, "I'll tell you a secret the Stoics knew. Your body is like a house, and you are the person living inside it. Sometimes the house needs repairs. It might feel pinchy or strange, but the 'you' inside is always safe."

Julian closed his eyes and used his Stoic Timeline. He imagined a long line: on the far left, "Today's Breakfast." In the middle, "Dentist Chair." On the far right, "Saturday Morning Cartoons."

This feeling in the chair is just a tiny dot on the line, he thought. In one hour, it will be in the past. It's already moving away.

When Dr. Aris began to work, Julian felt a sharp pinch. His Fire wanted to flare up. He wanted to jump out of the chair. But he stayed in his Gap.

This is just a sensation in the house, he whispered. It is not me. And it is already becoming the past.

He focused on his breathing—slow and steady, like a calm sea. He realized that the storm of worry before the chair had been louder than the work itself.

"All done, Captain!" Dr. Aris said, swinging the light away.

Julian sat up. The pinchy feeling was already fading. Something else wasn't fading: The warm pride in his chest.

The discomfort was temporary, but his calm and bravery felt like a permanent upgrade to his character. He walked out feeling taller. A Stoic doesn't have to be someone who never feels pain. A Stoic is someone who knows pain is a guest who doesn't stay long, while courage is a friend who can live there forever.

💭 What the Stoics Would Say

Seneca suffered from many illnesses, so he knew about physical discomfort. He wrote:

"Pain is slight if opinion has added nothing to it."

He meant that if we don't tell ourselves, "This is terrible, I can't stand it," the feeling is easier to handle. Our opinion is what makes the pain feel huge. When we keep our opinion calm, the body often follows.

🧠 Stoic Superpower

- **The Timeline Trick:** When you're in a moment that feels bad, imagine yourself an hour in the future looking back. Tell yourself, "This will soon be a memory."
- **The House and the Resident:** Say, "My body is the house; I am the person inside. The house might feel a pinch, but I am okay."
- **The Brave Breath:** Use your breath as an anchor. No matter what is happening to your tooth or your knee, you are still the boss of your breathing.

🔍 Your Turn to Reflect

- Can you remember a time you had to do something uncomfortable, like getting a shot or removing a splinter?
- Was the worrying before the event scarier than the event itself? Why do you think that is?
- How does it feel to know your courage stays with you even after the "ouch" is gone?

Chapter 17

The Messy Bedroom (Breaking Big Worries into Small Manageable Pieces)

Grace stood in her doorway and didn't see a floor. She saw a mountain.

A mountain made of mismatched socks, open books, plastic blocks, and half-finished drawings. Her mom said she couldn't go to the park until the room was clean. A heavy storm of overwhelm swirled in her stomach.

I can't do this, she thought. It's too much. It would take a million years.

Grace felt like a Captain staring at a hundred-foot wave. The mess felt so big her brain wanted to shut down. Instead of cleaning, she sat on the bed and started to cry. The more she stared at the whole mess, the more impossible it seemed.

Her older brother, Leo, poked his head in. He saw the piles and her face.

"Whoa," he said. "The storm hit this room hard, huh?"

"It's too big," Grace sobbed. "I don't even know where the floor is."

"You're trying to move the whole ocean at once," Leo said, sitting on a pile of stuffed animals. "No Captain can do that. You're looking at the Everything. A Stoic looks at the Now."

He picked up a single red sock and handed it to her.

"Can you put this one sock in the hamper?"

Grace blinked. "Well… yeah. That's easy." She dropped it in.

"Great," Leo said. "Now, just the Lego bricks. Don't worry about books or drawings. Just the Legos."

Grace picked up the bricks. Click, clack, click. In a few minutes, the Legos were in their bin. The mountain looked a tiny bit smaller.

"Now just the books," Leo said.

As Grace stacked books on the shelf, she noticed something: the storm in her stomach was gone. Why? Because she had stopped worrying about the finished room (which lived in the future) and started focusing on the single action (which lived in the present).

She stopped seeing a giant monster mess and started seeing small, easy jobs. One sock. One toy. One book. She was a Captain steering through one wave at a time, instead of trying to leap over the whole ocean.

Half an hour later, Grace stood in the doorway again. She saw her rug, her desk, her floor. But more importantly, she felt like the master of her own mind.

No task is too big if you break it into pieces small enough to carry.

💬 What the Stoics Would Say

Marcus Aurelius had a secret for getting things done. He wrote:

"Assemble your life one action at a time... no one can prevent you from doing that."

He meant you don't have to build a whole house in one second. You just have to lay one brick, then another. If you focus only on the brick in your hand, you don't feel crushed by how big the wall is.

🧠 Stoic Superpower

- **The "One Brick" Rule:** When a job looks too big, stop looking at the whole thing. Ask, "What is one small thing I can do right now?"
- **The "Now" Filter:** Anxiety lives in Later. Calm lives in Now. If you feel overwhelmed, your mind is probably too far ahead. Gently pull it back to the very next step.
- **The "Shrink" Trick:** Imagine the big worry is a giant balloon. Each small task is a tiny poke. Eventually, the giant worry shrinks into a flat bit of rubber.

🔍 Your Turn to Reflect

- Is there a chore or project that feels like a mountain to you right now?
- What is the smallest, easiest single action you could take to start?
- Why does it feel better to do one small thing than to sit and worry about the whole big thing?

Chapter 18

The Invisible Audience (Realizing Others Aren't Judging Us)

Sam was having a great Tuesday until the Mustard Disaster.

A tiny slip of a hot dog left a bright yellow streak in the middle of his white T-shirt. To Sam, that streak felt like a glowing sign: LOOK AT SAM! HE IS A MESS!

Walking from the cafeteria to class, Sam felt a storm of social anxiety. He crossed his arms over his chest to hide the spot. He felt like he was on a stage under a giant spotlight.

Every time kids laughed, he was sure they were laughing at his shirt. Every time a teacher looked his way, he was sure they were thinking how sloppy he was.

The Invisible Audience is watching, he thought. Everyone is judging me.

He ducked into the library to hide. There he saw his friend Susy staring at her fingernails, looking worried.

"Susy," Sam whispered, still covering his chest. "Does everyone know? Are they talking about it?"

"Talking about what?" she asked.

"My shirt!" He pointed to the yellow streak. "The disaster!"

Susy leaned in. "Oh. I didn't even see that," she said. "I was too busy worrying that everyone was staring at my hair. I tried to cut my bangs, and now I look like a lopsided hedge."

Sam looked at her hair. It was a bit uneven, but he hadn't noticed at all. He'd been too focused on his "mustard spotlight."

Suddenly, he realized the Stoic secret: there is no audience.

He looked around. One kid chewed a pencil, frowning at a report. Another checked her shoes for mud. Everyone was the main character in their own movie, and in their movies, they were under the spotlight.

They didn't have time to be the audience for Sam's movie, because they were too busy starring in their own.

Sam let out a big breath. The storm in his chest almost vanished. He uncrossed his arms. He realized the Invisible Audience was just a ghost he'd invented.

"You look fine, Susy," Sam said, sitting down. "And if anyone notices my shirt or your hair, that's just a thought in their head, not a problem in ours."

He spent the rest of the day with his arms uncrossed. He even forgot the mustard was there. When you stop performing for an audience that isn't even watching, you're finally free to be yourself.

💭 What the Stoics Would Say

Epictetus taught that it's often not the thing itself that upsets us, but the way we think about it.

"It is not things themselves that disturb us, but our judgments about them."

Sam's mustard stain was just a small spot on a shirt. What made it feel huge was the story in his head—that everyone was staring, judging, and talking about him. Once he realized that the story might not be true, the stain stopped feeling like a disaster.

🧠 Stoic Superpower

- **The Spotlight Switch:** When you feel like everyone is watching you, remind yourself, "Everyone here is the star of their own movie." They're mostly worrying about themselves.
- **The "So What?" Shield:** Ask, "If they notice my mistake, does it change who I am?" A mustard stain doesn't change your kindness, effort, or brain.
- **Look Outward:** Instead of staring at your own "spotlight," notice others. Many of them look nervous, too. Being kind to them turns down your own anxiety.

🔍 Your Turn to Reflect

- Can you remember a time you felt like "everyone" was looking at a mistake you made? Did anyone actually say anything?
- Why do our own mistakes feel much bigger to us than to other people?
- Next time you feel the Invisible Audience, can you imagine that everyone has their own little "mustard stain" they're worrying about?

Chapter 19

The Tomorrow-Worrier (Staying in the Present Moment)

It was a beautiful Sunday afternoon. The sun was golden, the backyard smelled like cut grass, and Peter's dad had just set up the sprinkler for water tag. But Peter wasn't running. He sat on the porch steps, staring at his toes.

Inside Peter's head, it was already Monday morning.

Tomorrow is the spelling bee, he thought. What if I get a word I've never heard of? What if I trip on the stage? What if my throat gets dry and I can't speak?

Even though the sun was warm on his back, Peter felt cold and shivery. Even though his sister was laughing in the sprinkler, he felt like he was drowning in a storm that hadn't arrived yet. He was a time-traveler, but only to the scary parts of the future.

His dad handed him a cold glass of lemonade. "You're not here, Peter," Dad said.

"What do you mean? I'm sitting right here," Peter said.

"Your body is on the porch," Dad said, "but your mind is in the school auditorium tomorrow. You're trying to fight a battle that hasn't started yet. And while you fight tomorrow's ghosts, you're missing today's sunshine."

Dad pulled a metal nut from his pocket and tied it to a string. "This is an Anchor. When a Captain sees a storm in the distance, he doesn't sail out to meet it. He drops his anchor where he is. He stays in the safe harbor until it's time to sail."

"How do I drop an anchor in my brain?" Peter asked.

"Use your senses," Dad replied. "The future is a thought; the Now is real. Tell me three things you can feel right now."

Peter took a breath. "The cold glass in my hand," he said. "The sun on my neck. The fuzzy feeling of my socks."

"Good. Now two things you can hear."

"The sprinkler clicking," he said. "A bird chirping in the oak tree."

As Peter focused on the cold glass and the clicking sprinkler, the storm of tomorrow started to fade. Tomorrow-Peter would have his brain, notes, and courage to handle the spelling bee. Today-Peter's only job was to play water tag and drink lemonade.

Peter stood and dropped an imaginary anchor into the grass. He felt heavy, steady, and real.

"I'm back, Dad!" he shouted, running into the sprinkler. The icy water shocked him into a laugh. The spelling bee was still coming, but for the first time all day, Peter was exactly where he was supposed to be: right here, right now.

💭 What the Stoics Would Say

Seneca understood time-traveling worries very well. He wrote:

"What I advise you to do is not to be unhappy before the crisis comes… We are in the habit of exaggerating, or imagining, or anticipating sorrow."

He meant we often "suffer" twice: once when we worry in advance, and once when the thing actually happens. A Stoic chooses to deal with it only once—when it arrives. Until then, they stay anchored in the present.

🧠 Stoic Superpower

- **The 3-2-1 Anchor:** When your mind worries about tomorrow, find 3 things you can feel, 2 things you can hear, and 1 thing you can smell. This pulls your mind back into your body.
- **The "Not My Business" Rule:** Tell yourself, "Tomorrow's problems are not my business today."
- **The Time-Travel Alarm:** Every time you catch yourself saying "What if…", follow it with "Right now, I am…" (For example, "Right now, I am sitting on the porch.")

🔍 Your Turn to Reflect

- Do you ever "lose" your weekend because you're worried about school on Monday?
- When you worry about the future, does it help you solve the problem, or just make you tired?
- What is your favorite thing about the Right Now at this very moment?

Chapter 20

The Map That Changed (Being Flexible When Plans Fall Through)

Roxane was a Planner. She loved her glittery planner, color-coded markers, and the feeling of knowing exactly what would happen next. For her 10th birthday, she created a masterpiece: **The Ultimate Birthday Map.**

1:00 PM: Pizza Party at the Park.

2:00 PM: Giant Inflatable Obstacle Course.

3:00 PM: Double-Decker Strawberry Cake.

But on Saturday morning, the sky wasn't birthday-blue. It was swirling, charcoal gray. The wind whipped the trees, and rain came down in sheets.

Ring! The phone chirped. Mom picked up. "Oh… I see. Thank you for letting us know," she said quietly. She turned to Roxane. "Sweetheart, that was the party company. They said the inflatable course can't be set up in this wind. It's not safe."

The storm of disappointment slammed into Roxane's chest. She looked at her beautiful map. It felt useless now. *My whole birthday is ruined,* she thought. *The map says "Park," but we're stuck inside. The map says "Obstacle Course," but there isn't one. Everything is wrong.*

She felt like a Captain who'd lost her compass in the middle of the ocean. She wanted to crumple the map and hide under her bed.

Grandpa, visiting for the weekend, saw her at the window. He picked up her drawing.

"That's a beautiful map, Roxane," he said. "But a map is just a piece of paper. The sea doesn't have to follow your paper."

"But I worked so hard on it!" Roxane cried. "It's not fair!"

"Roxane," Grandpa said gently, "the Stoics had something called a **reserve clause**. It means they quietly add: '*...if nothing prevents me.*' You planned the park, *if nothing prevented you.* Today, the weather prevented you. A weak Captain gives up when the path is blocked. A Stoic Captain draws a new path."

He handed her a blank sheet and a purple marker. "The map has changed. The goal hasn't. The goal is to have fun with your friends. How do we get there now?"

Roxane took a deep breath—her Stoic Gap. She looked at the rain. It wasn't "ruining" her day; it was changing the *route* of her day. She started a **New Map.**

1:00 PM: Pizza Picnic on the Living Room Floor.

2:00 PM: Indoor Scavenger Hunt (The Great Treasure Search).

3:00 PM: Cake & "Build-Your-Own Obstacle Course" out of couch cushions.

By the time her friends arrived, the house was covered in handwritten clues and pillow-mountains. The scavenger hunt turned out more exciting than the original obstacle course, and everyone ended up sweaty and giggling.

At the end of the day, Roxane looked at her two maps: the perfect one that never happened, and the scribbly one full of arrows and changes.

She realized a map is just a plan. Real life is the sea. The sea will do what it does—but she could always redraw the map.

💭 What the Stoics Would Say

The Stoics often reminded themselves to add *"if nothing prevents me"* to their plans. They knew that some things—like weather or illness—are outside our control. By planning with this quiet Reserve Clause, they stayed ready to adapt rather than collapse when plans changed.

🧠 Stoic Superpower

- **The Reserve Clause:** In your mind, add "…if nothing prevents me" to your plans. "We'll have a park party—if nothing prevents us."

- **Goal vs. Path:** Ask, "What is my real goal?" (Fun with friends, learning, kindness.) If one path is blocked, find another path to the same goal.
- **The New Map:** When something big changes, draw (or imagine) a New Map with three different steps you *can* take now.

🔍 Your Turn to Reflect

- Can you remember a time when your plans got ruined by weather, illness, or something else? What happened?
- Looking back, was there another path to your real goal that you didn't see at first?
- How might it feel to start quietly adding "…if nothing prevents me" to your plans?

Part 3: The Mountain (Building Confidence & Courage)

The Inner Citadel: Building a fortress of character that nothing can shake.

Character is like a Mountain: it stays standing, no matter what the weather does around it. A Mountain doesn't run from the wind or melt in the sun—it stays strong and steady.

In this part of the book, you'll learn how to build your own Inner Citadel—a quiet fortress inside your mind where your courage lives. You'll see that being "brave" isn't about never feeling scared; it's about taking the right step and moving forward even when your legs are shaking.

Chapter 21

The First Day of School (Courage Isn't the Absence of Fear)

The hallway smelled like fresh wax and new sneakers, but to Mary it felt like the entrance to a dark cave. It was the first day of fifth grade at a brand new school.

Mary stood by the heavy blue doors, her backpack feeling as if it were filled with lead. Her stomach did backflips, and her hands were cold. She watched other kids laughing and high-fiving and felt like the only person in the world who was shaking.

I'm not brave, she thought, her eyes stinging. A brave person wouldn't be this scared. A brave person would just walk in and start talking. I'm a coward.

Her dad knelt next to her. "Mary, what do you think courage looks like?" he asked.

"It looks like being a superhero," she whispered. "It looks like not being afraid of anything."

Dad shook his head and pulled a small, smooth stone from his pocket—her Mountain Stone. "That's a fairy tale, Mary," he said. "Real courage isn't the absence of fear. If you aren't scared, you don't need courage. Courage is when your heart is thumping, your knees are shaking, and you decide to take the step anyway. The Mountain doesn't ask the wind to stop blowing; the Mountain just stays standing while the wind howls."

Mary looked at the blue doors. The wind of her fear was howling loudly, urging her to run back to the car. But she looked at the stone in her hand and realized she didn't have to wait for the fear to go away before she started her day. Fear was just a passenger in her boat—it didn't have to be the Captain.

She took a Stoic Breath—four seconds in, four seconds out.

"I'm still scared, Dad," Mary said.

"I know," he smiled. "That's how I know you're being brave."

Mary gripped her backpack straps, lifted her chin, and walked through the blue doors. Every step felt heavy, but with each one, the Mountain inside her grew a little taller. By the time she found her desk and said "Hi" to the girl next to her, the fear was still there, but it felt smaller—like a tiny breeze instead of a hurricane. She realized she didn't need to be fearless to be a Stoic; she just needed to be the boss of her feet.

💭 What the Stoics Would Say

Seneca knew everyone feels fear. He wrote:

"It is not because things are difficult that we do not dare; it is because we do not dare that they are difficult."

He meant the "first day" often feels like a giant mountain, mostly because we haven't started climbing it yet. Once you take the first step, the mountain starts to feel more like a hill. Bravery is simply daring to move, even when you feel small.

🧠 Stoic Superpower

- **The "And" Rule:** You can feel scared and be brave at the same time.
- **The Passenger Seat:** Imagine your fear as a noisy passenger in your car; it doesn't get to touch the steering wheel.
- **The First Step Focus:** Don't stare at the whole school year—just the next ten feet of hallway.

🔍 Your Turn to Reflect

- Think of a time you did something even though you were very scared.
- If you waited until you were "never scared" to try new things, how many would you do?
- Why is someone who is scared but does the right thing braver than someone who isn't scared at all?

Chapter 22

The Talent Show (Performing for Yourself, Not the Crowd)

Caleb had a secret talent: he was a wizard with a yo-yo. He could make the spinning plastic disk dance—"Walk the Dog," "Around the World," and his favorite, "The Eiffel Tower." In his garage, he felt like he was flying.

Backstage at the Northwood Elementary Talent Show, the yo-yo felt like a heavy rock in his pocket. Through the velvet curtains, Caleb heard the roar of the crowd. Sarah finished a gymnastics routine with three backflips. The audience went wild. Then a boy played an electric guitar solo that made the floor vibrate.

The Mountain in Caleb's mind felt like it was crumbling. *Compared to backflips and rock stars, my yo-yo is boring,* he thought. *What if they don't clap? What if they think I'm just a kid with a toy?*

His teacher, Mr. Aris, noticed his pale face.

"Caleb, you look like you're preparing for a battle, not a show," he said.

"Everyone is so much better," Caleb whispered. "I'm worried I won't get any applause."

"Let's look at the Mountain," Mr. Aris said. "You've practiced that Eiffel Tower trick a thousand times. When you did it yesterday in the gym, how did you feel?"

"I felt great," Caleb said. "I felt strong."

"And did you feel that way because of a crowd, or because you knew you had mastered a hard skill?"

"Because I did it right," Caleb answered.

"Exactly," Mr. Aris said. "The crowd is like the wind—it blows hot and cold, and you can't control it. But your **internal audience**? That's you. If you go out there and do your best Eiffel Tower, you've already won, even if the room is silent. You aren't performing for them; you're performing for the person you see in the mirror."

Caleb took a Stoic Breath. He realized he'd been trying to hand his happiness to the audience. He decided to keep it for himself instead.

When it was his turn, he walked onto the stage. The bright lights made it hard to see faces—perfect. He didn't search for the judges or his friends. He looked at the string in his hand.

Click, whirr, zip. He missed his first "Around the World," but instead of panicking, he gave a small, steady smile and kept going. He wasn't thinking, *Do they like me?* He was thinking, *I am doing the work I love.*

When he finally pulled the string to create the "Eiffel Tower," he held it perfectly steady for three long seconds. Pride shot from his toes to his head.

The audience did clap—loudly—but as Caleb walked off stage, he realized the clapping was just a bonus. The real prize was standing on his own Mountain, knowing he had done his best for the only person who truly has to approve: himself.

💭 What the Stoics Would Say

Marcus Aurelius wrote about how silly it is to worry about what people say about us. He said:

"Everything that is beautiful is beautiful in itself… it does not become better or worse by being praised."

A diamond is still a diamond even if no one says it's pretty Your effort and practice are "beautiful" because they are real, not because a crowd cheers for them.

🧠 Stoic Superpower

- **The Internal Audience:** Say, "I'm doing this to prove to myself that I can, not to prove it to them."
- **Applause Is a Bonus:** It's nice when people cheer for you, but you don't need it to feel proud of yourself.

- **Master the String:** Focus on the doing (string, steps, lines), not the result (trophy or claps).

🔍 Your Turn to Reflect

- Have you ever done something you were proud of, even though no one saw?
- Why is it risky to let other people decide if you are "good" or "bad" at something?
- What's one thing you love to do just for the joy of doing it, even without an audience?

Chapter 23

Learning to Ride
(Falling Is Just Data for Your Next Try)

Theo stood at the top of the driveway, glaring at his bike. The training wheels were gone, leaving the bike looking skinny and untrustworthy.

"Are you ready, Theo?" his dad asked, holding the back of the seat.

Theo nodded, heart thumping. He pushed off. For three glorious seconds, he was flying. Then the bike tilted. Theo panicked, oversteered left, and—THUD.

He landed in a heap on the grass. His knee stung, but his pride hurt more. *I'm a failure,* he thought. *I'm just not one of those kids who can ride.*

"I'm done," Theo muttered. "This bike is broken."

Dad sat on the grass next to him. "The bike isn't broken, Theo," he said. "And neither are you. You just received a very important delivery."

"A delivery? From who?" Theo asked.

"From the pavement," Dad said. "It just sent you a pile of **data**."

"Stoics look at the world like scientists," he explained. "When you fell, you didn't fail—you ran an experiment. The data says: 'If I lean too far left and don't pedal fast enough, the bike goes down.' That's not a sad story. It's just a fact. Now you know what to change for the next experiment."

Theo looked at his bike differently. Calling himself a "failure" had turned a simple event into a scary story. The fall itself wasn't good or bad; it was just information, like a note that said, *Try it another way.*

He stood, brushed off his jeans, and climbed back on.

Experiment Number Two, he thought.

When the bike tilted, he didn't panic. *Leaning left... okay, pedal faster... straighten the bars.* Five seconds. Six. When he tipped over again, he didn't cry. He just noted: *Need more speed to stay upright.*

By the end of the afternoon, Theo was riding all the way down the driveway. He still didn't *like* falling, but he had stopped using falls as proof that he "couldn't do it." Instead, each slip was a small note for his next try. The Mountain of Confidence wasn't built by never falling; it was built by getting up, reading the data, and trying again.

💭 What the Stoics Would Say

Epictetus told his students to be like athletes who get knocked down but always get back up. He said:

"When a guide sees someone who has gone off the path, he helps them find their way back instead of making fun of them."

Be your own kind guide. When you make a mistake, don't be harsh with yourself. Just pause, take a breath, and gently guide yourself back to the right path.

🧠 Stoic Superpower

- **The Little Scientist:** When you mess up, ask, "What data did I just get?"
- **Delete the Label:** Never say, "I am a failure." Only, "That attempt didn't work."
- **Next Experiment Mindset:** Don't stare at the fall. Focus on what you'll adjust on the very next try.

🔍 Your Turn to Reflect

- Think of something you're learning now that's hard. What data have your mistakes given you?
- Why is it easier to try again when a mistake is "information" instead of "failure"?
- How would you talk to a friend who fell off their bike? Can you talk to yourself that way?

Chapter 24

The "I Can't" Wall (Turning Obstacles Into The Way Forward)

Amara loved building castles, marble runs, and puzzles. If it involved pieces clicking together, she was in her happy place. But the Bridge Project was different. Her teacher had given them a challenge: build a bridge from toothpicks and glue that could hold a heavy dictionary. No tape. No cheating. Just sticks, patience, and a good design.

At first, Amara was excited. She drew a tall, fancy bridge with towers and flags. She carefully glued toothpicks into long lines and propped them up on two stacks of books. It looked amazing.

Then she tested it.

Every time she reached the middle, the toothpicks snapped. CRACK.

More glue. CRACK.

Double layers. CRACK.

The dictionary didn't even have to sit all the way down before the bridge sagged and broke. By Thursday night, Amara hit the "I Can't" Wall—a wall in her mind made of frustration and "I'm not smart enough." She shoved her chair back, cheeks hot and eyes stinging.

"I'm done!" she yelled. "The toothpicks are too weak. The glue is too slow. I can't do it!"

Her grandmother, a retired engineer, heard the crash and came in. She didn't rush to hug Amara or fix the bridge for her. Instead, she looked closely—not at Amara's angry face, but at the pile of snapped toothpicks on the table.

"Oh, how lucky!" Grandma said, smiling.

"Lucky?" Amara cried. "My bridge is a pile of splinters!"

"Because," Grandma said, picking up a broken piece, "the bridge just told you exactly where it's weak. Every break is a map. The obstacle isn't blocking you; it's teaching you how to build the real bridge."

She sat down beside Amara. "The Stoics had a secret," she added. "Whatever stands in your way can become the path you need to take. If the middle keeps breaking, that is where you need to get creative. The 'Wall' isn't there to stop you; it's there to make you a better builder."

Amara took a Stoic Breath and stepped into the Gap between her frustration and her next move. She decided to treat the snapped sticks as instructions, not insults.

If the middle is snapping, she thought, maybe I shouldn't just add more glue. Maybe I should change the shape to a triangle.

She experimented—shorter pieces, triangle patterns, crisscross supports. She let the problem guide the design instead of fighting it. By sundown, the bridge was a masterpiece of triangles and strength. When she placed the dictionary on top, it didn't even creak.

Amara realized the "I Can't" Wall had been a gift. Without it, she'd have built a weak, boring bridge. Because it broke, she had to grow. The obstacle didn't just stand in her way—it showed her the way forward.

💭 What the Stoics Would Say

Marcus Aurelius wrote:

"The impediment to action advances action. What stands in the way becomes the way."

That means when something blocks your path, you don't have to stop. You find a way to move through it, keep going and even grow stronger because of it.

🧠 Stoic Superpower

- **The Obstacle Flip:** When something goes wrong, ask, "How can this problem help me get better?"
- **The Power of Yet:** Never say, "I can't." Say, "I haven't figured it out yet."

- **The Triangle Test:** Find the "triangles" in your life—the strong habits and thoughts that keep you sturdy.

🔍 Your Turn to Reflect

- Is there a "Wall" you're hitting now—a hard level, a tricky piece, a chore?
- How could that "Wall" be a teacher in disguise?
- Why is someone who's overcome many obstacles usually stronger than someone who's never had problems?

Chapter 25

The Question in Class (The Bravery of Being Curious)

Omar was usually a Mountain of Silence in Mrs. Gable's math class. He liked to sit in the third row, blend into his blue chair, and hope he never got called on.

Today, Mrs. Gable was explaining equivalent fractions. One-half was the same as four-eighths. Heads were nodding. Pencils were moving.

Omar looked at his paper. The numbers looked like a jumbled mess of ants. He didn't understand why the bottom number changed, but the value didn't. A storm of panic rose.

If I ask a question, everyone will turn around, he thought. They'll think I'm the only one who doesn't get it. Better to pretend I know and just fail the quiz later.

He was letting an invisible audience steer his ship. He was choosing the easy path of staying confused instead of the rocky path of being brave.

Then Omar looked at a poster of a mountain climber reaching for a high ledge. He remembered: When you feel stuck, action is often the best medicine. He didn't have to wait for the storm in his stomach to stop before raising his hand. He could be scared and curious at the same time.

In the Stoic Gap, he asked: What's the goal of being in this room—to look like a genius or actually learn math?

The answer was clear. A Stoic wants the truth, even if it's a little embarrassing to get there.

Omar's heart did the Category 5 thump. His hand felt like it weighed a thousand pounds. But he took a breath and pushed it into the air.

"Mrs. Gable?" he said, voice squeaky. "I… I don't understand why the bottom number changes. Can you show that part again?"

The room went quiet. Omar braced for laughter.

Instead, he heard a sigh of relief from the girl next to him. "Oh, thank goodness," she whispered. "I was totally lost, too."

Mrs. Gable smiled. "I'm so glad you asked, Omar. That's the trickiest part," she said. She drew a giant pizza and explained it in a new way. Suddenly, the "ants" on Omar's paper turned into a picture he could understand.

By the end of the day, Omar didn't just feel smarter about fractions. He felt stronger. Every time you ask a question, you swing a pickaxe at the Mountain of Ignorance. Being curious didn't make him look small; it made him the bravest person in the third row.

💭 What the Stoics Would Say

Epictetus told his students that real learning matters more than looking smart. He reminded them that pretending to know everything only blocks growth. A true student would rather ask a simple question and understand than remain silent and confused.

The Stoics believed it is better to be a humble learner than a proud pretend-expert. When you raise your hand, you're choosing wisdom over worrying about what others think.

If you want to get better at math, sports, or being kind, you have to be okay with people noticing that you don't know something yet. You can't learn if you're too busy pretending you already know.

🧠 Stoic Superpower

- **The "Me Too" Rule:** If you're confused, at least three others probably are too.
- **Truth Over Trinkets:** Your education is a treasure; don't trade it just to look cool for five minutes.
- **The Five-Second Hand:** When you have a question, don't think for more than five seconds— lift your hand.

🔍 Your Turn to Reflect

- Have you stayed silent because you didn't want to look "silly"? How did you feel later?
- Why do teachers actually love "basic" questions?
- If you could ask one brave question tomorrow, what would it be?

Chapter 26

The Secret Skill (Confidence Comes from Doing the Work)

Ricky stared at the grand piano on the stage. In four days, he was supposed to play "Moonlight Sonata" at the Spring Recital. His storm of anxiety swirled. What if I mess up in front of everyone? What if my hands shake? What if I forget the notes?

He watched his classmate, Chloe, practice. She looked relaxed. Her fingers danced without a stumble. When she finished, she hopped off the bench, laughing, like the piano was a friend, not a test.

"I wish I had her confidence," Ricky sighed to his teacher, Mr. H. "Chloe was born brave. I'm born nervous. I'm waiting for that 'confident feeling' to hit me, but it hasn't."

"Do you know how she got that 'brave' look?" Mr. H asked. "She didn't find it in a gift box."

"Then where did it come from?"

"It's a secret skill called **competence**," Mr. H said. "That just means knowing how to do something because you've practiced. Confidence is what grows from that. Chloe isn't just 'feeling' brave; she's remembering that she has practiced that song three hundred times. Her fingers know the way, so her mind can be at peace."

Ricky looked at his music. He'd only practiced the hard middle part about ten times. No wonder he didn't feel sure.

"So I don't have to wait for the feeling?" he asked.

"No," Mr. H said. "If you wait for the feeling, you might wait forever. A Stoic doesn't wait for the feeling to start the work. They do the work to make the feeling show up."

Ricky took a Stoic Breath and stepped into the Gap. He didn't try to feel like a master pianist. He just decided to be the **Master of the Next Five Minutes**.

He practiced the middle section—slowly at first, then a little faster. Then again. Then ten more times. His hands got tired. It was boring. Sometimes he wanted to slam the lid shut and quit. But each time he slipped, he circled the wrong bar and played it again, treating every mistake as information, not proof that he was "no good."

By the third day, something strange happened. As he sat down at the piano, he didn't feel a storm in his stomach. He felt… solid. His fingers knew exactly where to go. He had traded worry for work, and the trade was paying off.

On recital night, Ricky walked onto the stage. He still had a tiny bit of jitters, but he didn't let them steer. He sat, looked at the keys, and let his competence take over. The "Secret Skill" wasn't something he was born with. It lived in all the quiet hours he had spent practicing when no one was watching.

💭 What the Stoics Would Say

Epictetus had a simple formula:

"If you want to be a writer, write."

He didn't say, "Wait until you feel like a writer." You become something by doing its actions. If you want to be confident at anything, practice that thing—again and again.

🧠 Stoic Superpower

- **The Competence Loop:** When you feel "unconfident," ask, "How many times have I actually done this?"
- **The "Do It First" Rule:** Don't wait for the perfect mood to start. Moods change all the time, like sunny days and rainy days. Habits are different. Habits stay steady, like a mountain. It doesn't move every time the wind blows.
- **The 10-Rep Rule:** If you're scared of a task, do ten small repetitions.

🔍 Your Turn to Reflect

- What's something you want to be confident at? How many times have you practiced it this week?

- Why is it good that we have to work for confidence instead of getting it for free?
- Think of something you're good at now—do you remember when you weren't? What changed?

Chapter 27

Standing Up for Sam
(The Courage to Be Just When It's Hard)

Elena sat at the Circle Table in the cafeteria. This was where the "popular kids" sat, and she had worked hard to be invited. It felt like a sunny plateau on her social Mountain, high above the noisy valley of the lunchroom.

Today, the sun wasn't shining. Toby, the unofficial leader, pointed at Sam, who sat alone two tables away. Sam was new, a bit quiet, and wearing a sweater with a giant, colorful solar system.

"Check out Space Boy," Toby snickered. "Hey, Sam! Is Mars as lonely as you are?"

The table erupted in laughter. Elena felt a sharp, cold storm in her chest. She liked Sam—they'd worked together in science, and he'd explained black holes to her in a way that actually made sense. She knew Toby was being cruel, not clever.

At the same time, she felt the fire of fear. If I say something, Toby will turn the spotlight on me, she thought. I'll get kicked off the Circle Table.

Elena stared at her tray, her heart pounding. She stood in the Stoic Gap. On one side was the easy path—stay quiet, keep her seat, pretend she didn't hear. On the other was the rocky path—stand up for Justice and risk losing her "place."

She remembered something she'd read: Justice is the soul's health. If she stayed silent, she'd be letting Toby poison her character just to keep a seat. The Circle Table wasn't a real Mountain; it was a pile of sand that could blow away with the next rumor or joke. The only solid Mountain was her integrity.

Elena took a breath. Her hands shook under the table, but her voice came out steady.

"Actually, Toby," she said loudly, "I think the sweater is cool. And Sam is a lot more interesting than a bunch of people making fun of clothes."

The laughter stopped. Trays paused in midair. Toby stared.

"You're defending Space Boy?" he scoffed. "You want to go sit with him?"

"I'd rather sit with a friend than with a bully," Elena said.

She picked up her tray. Every eye felt like a spotlight on her back. Her heart thumped so hard she could hear it in her ears, but she didn't look down. She walked to Sam's table and sat.

"Nice sweater, Sam," she said once her voice stopped shaking.

"Thanks, Elena," Sam whispered, his face bright with surprise and relief. "That was... really brave."

They started talking about planets and favorite movies. The Circle Table buzzed behind them, but it sounded farther away now, like a storm moving off in the distance.

Elena realized that by standing up for Sam, she'd done something better than being "popular." She'd built a piece of her Inner Citadel—a strong stone room of Justice—that Toby could never touch or knock down.

💭 What the Stoics Would Say

Marcus Aurelius believed his most important job was to be just. He wrote:

"If it is not right, do not do it; if it is not true, do not say it."

Justice is simple. Check your inner compass. If something feels wrong in your heart, it's wrong—no matter how many people are laughing.

🧠 Stoic Superpower

- **The Integrity Compass:** Ask, "If I were the only person on earth, would I think this is okay?"
- **The Seat Swap:** If being in a group requires unkindness, that group is a storm, not a harbor.

- **The Justice Shield:** Others can control where you sit, but only you control whether you are a good person.

🔍 Your Turn to Reflect

- Have you ever seen someone treated unfairly and felt afraid to speak up?
- Why does it feel better, in the long run, to sit alone and be just than to sit with a crowd and be unjust?
- How could you show Justice to someone being ignored or teased this week?

Chapter 28

The Solo Hike (Finding Strength in Being Alone With Your Thoughts)

Jada loved a loud crew—her tablet, her music, her friends. Silence felt like a glitched screen: empty and boring. If the house was quiet, she reached for headphones. If no one was texting, she opened a game. Being alone with her own thoughts felt like being stuck in an elevator between floors.

At summer camp, there was a rule: the Solo Ten. For ten minutes every afternoon, each camper had to sit alone on Observation Hill—no phone, no book, no friend, no talking. Just you, the hill, and your mind.

On Tuesday, Jada sat on a flat gray rock. The storm of restlessness hit right away. Her legs wanted to fidget. Her fingers twitched, reaching for a screen that wasn't there. Her brain begged for a video, a song, or a person to talk to. This is a waste of time, she thought. It's too quiet.

She felt the fire of annoyance. The other campers looked like statues, scattered across the hill. Jada felt like a ship lost in fog with no lighthouse, nothing to do, nowhere to go.

Then she remembered the Mountain lesson. A Mountain doesn't need a crowd to be tall. It doesn't need music to be strong. It just is.

She decided to stop fighting the silence and start exploring it. She closed her eyes and stepped into the Stoic Gap. Instead of hunting for something to do, she began noticing what was happening inside her own Inner Citadel.

She noticed her breathing—the small ocean in her chest, rising and falling. She noticed a thought about her dog pop up, and watched it drift by like a cloud without chasing it. She noticed the scritch-scritch of a beetle in the grass, the far-off shout from the lake, the smell of warm pine needles, and the solid rock beneath her legs.

Time started to feel different. The ten minutes weren't a punishment anymore; they were an invitation.

Suddenly, Jada realized a secret: she wasn't really alone—she was with herself. Her mind wasn't a boring, empty room; it was a library of memories, a workshop of ideas, and a fortress where she could rest. She didn't need a screen to entertain her; she had a whole universe inside her head.

The storm of restlessness settled into a quiet Mountain of peace.

When the counselor blew the whistle, Jada didn't jump up. She sat three extra seconds, enjoying the quiet. Walking back down the hill, she felt a new kind of strength. Being alone didn't make her lonely; it made her self-reliant. She knew that wherever she went—busy city, noisy classroom, or empty room—she could always hike back into the calm Mountain inside herself.

💭 What the Stoics Would Say

Marcus Aurelius believed we all have a quiet place inside us. He wrote:

"Look within. Inside you is a fountain of good, and it will keep bubbling up if you keep digging for it."

This means that courage, peace, and goodness do not have to come from outside you. You don't need a vacation to find peace. You can retreat into your own mind by sitting still and breathing. Your mind is the one place where you are always the boss.

🧠 Stoic Superpower

- **The Five-Sense Scan:** When bored or lonely, name 5 things you see, 4 you feel, 3 you hear, 2 you smell, 1 you can taste.
- **The Thought Cloud Game:** Imagine thoughts as clouds passing over your Mountain; name them and let them drift.
- **The Inner Library:** Tell yourself, "I am my own best friend. I have stories, memories, and ideas only I can see."

🔍 Your Turn to Reflect

- When was the last time you sat in silence for five minutes? How did it feel?
- Why do we often feel we must always be doing or talking?
- If you were on a deserted island, what three things about you would still make you a strong Mountain?

Chapter 29

The Mistake on Stage (Owning Your Errors with a Stoic Smile)

The gym was packed. Every chair was filled, and people stood at the back and along the walls. The air buzzed with whispers and the squeak of folding chairs. Marcus played the lead in *The Legend of the Brave Knight.* He had practiced his lines until he could say them in his sleep, in the shower, and while brushing his teeth.

Backstage, he'd felt only a small flutter. I've got this, he told himself. I know every word.

Then the white spotlight hit his face.

Under that hot circle of light, the storm arrived. Marcus walked to the center of the stage for his big speech about courage. This was the moment everyone had been waiting for.

He opened his mouth—and nothing came out.

His mind went blank, like someone had wiped his script clean with an eraser. The fire of embarrassment rushed up his neck into his cheeks. The silence felt heavy, like a big rock sitting in the gym. A few kids in the front row whispered. Someone coughed. Somewhere, a program rustled.

I'm ruining the play, he thought. Everyone will remember the knight who forgot how to talk.

For a second, he wanted to bolt off stage, hide behind the curtain, and never come back. But he didn't move. He took a Stoic Breath and stepped into the Gap. The mistake had already happened. That part of time was over. He couldn't change the past. He could only choose the next second.

Instead of staring at his feet and wishing to disappear, Marcus did something unexpected.

He took a deeper breath, lifted his chin, looked right at the audience, and gave a small, calm Stoic Smile.

"Even a knight," he said, improvising with a tiny wink, "sometimes needs a moment to remember the map."

There was a pause—and then the audience chuckled. Not a mean laugh at him, but a warm laugh with him. The storm in his chest cracked open. His muscles loosened. As if someone flipped a switch, his real lines rushed back into his mind. He finished the speech with more energy than ever, sword held high.

After the play, people didn't crowd around to whisper about the forgotten line. They talked about how "professional" he'd been. His teacher said, "You handled that like a real actor." His friends said, "That little joke was awesome."

Marcus realized perfection is like a glass vase—it looks nice but breaks easily. Poise is like the Mountain—solid, steady, still standing even after a storm. When he smiled at his mistake and kept going, he showed he was the boss of his feelings, not their prisoner.

💭 What the Stoics Would Say

Epictetus taught that we shouldn't be ruled by fear of looking silly. He said:

"If you want to improve, be content to be thought foolish and silly."

Everyone who's learning will look awkward sometimes. If you're too afraid of that, you'll never do anything great. Other people's giggles don't decide your worth. Owning your mistake with a smile says, "My value doesn't come from being perfect; it comes from being honest and brave."

🧠 Stoic Superpower

- **The Stoic Smile:** When you mess up, give a small smile to show the mistake hasn't broken you.
- **The "So What?" Test:** Ask, "Will anyone remember this in a week?" If not, don't let it ruin your minute.
- **Improvisation:** If you slip, don't freeze—find a simple way to keep going.

🔍 Your Turn to Reflect

- Have you seen someone make a mistake and handle it with a laugh or calm attitude? Did you respect them more or less?
- Why does getting angry or crying about a mistake usually make things feel worse?
- How can you practice "owning the error" the next time you get an answer wrong?

Chapter 30

The Giant Leap
(Doing the Right Thing Because It Is Right)

Pete was at the Summer Fun Fair. The air smelled like popcorn and cotton candy, and bells, music, and cheering filled the air from every direction. He had five dollars left—just enough for one last ride on the Sky Screamer, the tallest ride in the park. He'd been saving that ride for the grand finale.

As he walked toward the line, weaving through people with balloons and dripping ice cream cones, something shiny near the trash cans caught his eye. He bent down and picked up a thick leather wallet.

Inside were three twenty-dollar bills and a ten. Seventy dollars. Enough for ten rides, a giant stuffed panda, and a mountain of fudge.

He looked around. The fair was crowded. Kids ran past, adults chatted, lights flashed. No one had seen him pick it up. The Fire of temptation whispered, *It's your lucky day. Finders keepers. Think of all the fun you could have.*

Pete stood at the base of one of his biggest Mountains. On one side, he felt the pull of the easy path—keep the money, buy tickets, and have an amazing afternoon. On the other, he felt the quiet tug of his Captain's Compass.

He checked it: *If I keep this, what kind of person am I becoming?*

He imagined himself on the Sky Screamer, wind in his face, stomach flipping—and a heavy rock sitting in his chest. If he kept it, he might have a fun hour, but he'd carry that heavy feeling much longer. He would know he had taken what wasn't his.

Pete took a Stoic Breath. Doing the right thing wasn't a tiny step; it was a **giant leap**—from doing what feels good to doing what *is* good.

He turned away from the Sky Screamer and walked to the security booth.

"I found this by the trash cans," he said, handing over the wallet.

The officer opened it, checked the ID, and his eyes widened. "This belongs to one of the elderly volunteers at the petting zoo," he said. "She's been looking everywhere for it. Thank you for bringing it in."

He offered Pete an "Honesty" sticker. Pete took it and stuck it on his shirt, but on the way to the gate, he realized he didn't need it to know what he'd done. His last five dollars went to a hot dog and a bottle of water instead of a giant ride, and that was okay. There was no surprise prize, no extra tickets, no big speech—just a quiet, solid feeling in his chest.

He had done the right thing, not for a reward and not from fear of getting in trouble, but simply because it was right. A horse doesn't ask for a trophy for running; a bee doesn't ask for a medal for making honey. They do what they were made to do.

Pete had acted like a human being of character. That knowledge—*I did the right thing when no one was watching*—was a strength he could carry out of the fair and into every day of his life.

💭 What the Stoics Would Say

Marcus Aurelius believed being good should be as natural as breathing. He wrote:

"A man who has done a good deed... does not shout it from the rooftops... he passes on to the next act, just as a vine produces another bunch of grapes in the right season."

You shouldn't do good for applause. You should do it because that's what your soul was built for. Being a good person is the prize.

🧠 Stoic Superpower

- **The Mirror Test:** Before a choice, ask, "Will I be proud of the person in the mirror tonight?"
- **Vine and Grapes Rule:** Do one good thing today and tell no one about it. Let your character be the only witness.

- **Virtue Is the Prize:** Say, "I don't do the right thing to get something. I do the right thing to be someone."

🔍 Your Turn to Reflect

- Have you ever found something that wasn't yours? What did you do?
- Why does it feel "heavy" inside when we do something we know is wrong, even if no one finds out?
- If someone offered you a huge prize to be mean to a friend, would you do it? What does your Captain's Compass say about that?

Part 4: The Anchor (Finding Gratitude & Contentment)

Amor Fati: Learning to love your fate, even the "boring" or "bad" parts, because they make you who you are.

Imagine your happiness is a boat. If it isn't anchored, it drifts away every time the wind blows or the waves get choppy. Gratitude is the **anchor** that keeps you steady.

The Stoics practiced something called Amor Fati, which translates to 'Love your Fate.' It means that instead of wishing for a different life, you learn to love the one you have—the rainy days, the old toys, and the quiet moments—because every part of your life is a gift that helps make you who you are.

Chapter 31

The Rain on the Picnic Day (Finding the Fun in the Puddles)

Julie had been counting down the minutes until Saturday. Her family was going to Pine Lake for the Big Summer Picnic. She had her swimsuit ready, the watermelon was sliced, and she could already taste the grilled corn. In her notebook, she had even drawn a little map of the day: *swim, eat, explore, repeat.*

But when she woke up, she didn't hear birds. She heard a steady patter-patter-patter on the roof. The sky outside her window was the color of a wet sidewalk.

"The one day we have a picnic, and it rains," Julie groaned. "My whole Saturday is ruined."

Her dad walked in, wearing his yellow raincoat and holding his phone. "Well," he said, "the lake is a no-go. The ranger says the trails are all mud and the water level is too high."

"Great," Julie muttered, flopping back onto her pillow. "Everything is terrible."

"Is it?" Dad asked, sitting on the edge of the bed. "The trees are getting a long drink. The frogs are probably having a party. The rain isn't 'bad'—it's just happening. We can spend the day mad at the clouds, or we can practice **Amor Fati**."

"Love the rain?" Julie made a face. "How am I supposed to love something that ruined my picnic?"

"By treating it as *today's* material," Dad said. "A great Captain doesn't only sail in sunshine. They use whatever weather they get. What if, instead of fighting the rain, we invite it into the plan?"

Julie stared at the window. The drops raced each other down the glass. She felt the Storm of Disappointment in her chest… but also a tiny spark of curiosity.

She took a slow breath. She looked at the rain again. It wasn't an enemy anymore; it was the background music for a new kind of Saturday.

"Could we make an 'Indoor Forest' picnic—build a fort, use green blankets for grass, and watch a rainforest movie while we eat our watermelon?" she asked.

Dad's eyes lit up. "Now you're loving your fate," he laughed. "I'll grab the blankets. You're in charge of fort design."

They spent the next half hour turning the living room into a forest. Green blankets became mossy ground. Chairs and broomsticks held up a tent roof. Flashlights shone through pillow "leaves," making little patches of pretend sunlight.

Julie put on her swimsuit anyway—under her T-shirt—just because it felt fun. They spread out the watermelon and grilled corn on a big towel. On the TV, parrots and monkeys chattered in a rainforest.

The watermelon tasted just as sweet on the living-room floor as it would have at the lake. Julie realized something important: the rainy Saturday wasn't a mistake; it was a different kind of gift.

Outside, the rain kept falling. Inside, Julie felt calm and happy.

A Stoic doesn't wait for the weather to change; they learn to **love** the weather they get.

💭 What the Stoics Would Say

Cleanthes, one of the early Stoics said:

"Fate guides the willing, but drags the unwilling."

He meant that some things, like rain, surprises, traffic, or cancellations, are going to happen whether we scream or not, so we suffer less when we choose to walk with them rather than be dragged.

🧠 Stoic Superpower

- **The Amor Fati Flip:** When something "bad" happens, ask: "How can I make this the best thing that happened today?"
- **The "Happening" Rule:** Say, "This isn't happening to me; it's just happening."

- **The Puddle Jump:** If you can't change the situation, change your shoes and find a way to play in the "puddles."

🔍 Your Turn to Reflect

- When has a "bad" change of plans turned into a fun memory?
- Why is it exhausting to stay angry at things like the weather or flat tires?
- What "boring" or "bad" thing in your life could you try to love this week?

Chapter 32

The Lost Favorite Shirt (Nothing Is Truly Ours; It's Only "On Loan")

Glenn had a shirt that made him feel like a superhero—soft, faded blue, with a small lightning bolt on the pocket. He wore it to every big event. Soccer games. School plays. Family parties. If something important was happening, the Lucky Shirt had to be there.

When he put it on, he felt braver, faster, and a little bit cooler. It wasn't just a shirt. It was part of who he was.

After a camping weekend with his family, Glenn dumped his backpack onto his bedroom floor. Out tumbled socks, granola bar wrappers, a flashlight… but no shirt.

He frowned and checked again. Backpack: empty. Car seats: checked. Under the seats: checked again. The tent bag, the duffel, the laundry basket. Nothing.

They even called the ranger station.

"Sorry, kid," the ranger said over the phone. "We don't have any lost-and-found shirts here."

By dinnertime, Glenn was a storm cloud.

"I can't be 'Lucky Glenn' without that shirt," he said, stabbing his broccoli. "It was mine. The universe shouldn't have taken it."

Mom handed him a glass of water and sat down. "Imagine I lent you my favorite book for a week," she said. "When I ask for it back, would you be angry?"

"No," Glenn said. "It was yours. I was just borrowing it."

Mom nodded. "The Stoics believed the whole world is like that. Your shirt, your bike, your toys—none of them belong to us forever. The universe lends them to us for a while. When they're lost or broken, we're not being 'robbed'; we're just returning them."

Glenn stared at the table. He realized he had been holding onto the shirt so tightly in his mind that losing it felt like losing a piece of himself.

"So I was just borrowing the lightning bolt?" he asked quietly.

"Exactly," Mom said. "You wore it for two years and had all kinds of adventures in it. Instead of being mad that the loan is over, can you be grateful you had it at all?"

Glenn thought about soccer goals, birthday cake, and campfires—all in that shirt. He took a slow breath. "I guess… I did get a lot of good days out of it."

He realized something else, too. "Lucky Glenn" wasn't hiding inside the blue fabric. The courage wasn't sewn into the pocket.

It was inside him the whole time. The shirt had just been a guest.

That night, before bed, Glenn stood by his window and whispered into the dark, "Thank you, shirt, for two years of fun. You can go be a rag or a bird's nest now."

The sadness didn't disappear, but it softened. If everything is on loan, then every day he has something is a bonus day.

The next morning, he pulled on a plain gray T-shirt and went outside. The sky was bright, the grass was wet, and the soccer ball waited in the yard.

He took a running start and kicked it hard. The ball flew just as far as ever.

He smiled. He didn't need a lightning bolt on his chest to be himself.

💭 What the Stoics Would Say

Epictetus said:

"Never say about anything, 'I have lost it,' but only 'I have given it back.'"

Enjoy your things, friends, and time, but remember you don't own the world. When everything is a temporary gift, you fear less and feel more grateful.

🧠 Stoic Superpower

- **The "Return" Phrase:** When you lose or break something, say, "I have returned this to the world."
- **The Guest Mindset:** Treat favorite items like guests—kindness while they're here, no despair when they leave.
- **Inner Power Check:** Ask yourself, "If I lost all my stuff, could I still choose to be kind and brave?"

🔍 Your Turn to Reflect

- What's one "lucky" or favorite item you'd be sad to lose?
- How would it feel to think, "I'm glad the world is lending this to me today"?
- Why is it better to be happy with a little than to only be happy when you have everything?

Chapter 33

The Power of "Enough" (Gratitude for What We Already Have)

Zara lay on the floor with a toy catalog spread open in front of her. On the center page was the thing every kid at school was talking about—the new Glow-Bots. Shiny, color-changing, voice-recording robots with tiny wheels and glowing eyes.

"They can dance, record your voice, and follow you around the room," the ad said. The Glow-Bots in the picture looked like tiny, friendly space explorers.

Zara glanced over at her wooden blocks and her stuffed rabbit, Fluffy. The blocks were chipped in places, and Fluffy's ear flopped over where the stitching had come loose. Suddenly, they looked dull and old.

"I need a Glow-Bot," Zara declared. "If I had one, I'd be the happiest kid in the galaxy. My room is boring without it."

Her uncle Marcus, who was visiting for a few weeks, looked up from the chair. He was a traveler who lived out of one backpack and had been all over the world.

"That's a very bright robot," he said, leaning over to look. "How many Glow-Bots would it take to make you feel full?"

"Just one!" Zara said quickly. Then she paused. "Okay… maybe two so they can talk to each other."

Uncle Marcus smiled. "The Stoics warned that wanting more is like drinking salt water. The more you drink, the thirstier you get. If you never learn 'Enough,' you can be a beggar in a palace."

Zara frowned. "A beggar? I have a bed and a roof. I'm not poor."

"Exactly," he replied. "You already have the big things—bed, brain, Fluffy." He nodded toward her stuffed rabbit. "If you wait for a robot to bring joy, you're giving your power to plastic."

Zara looked back at the catalog. The Glow-Bots still looked cool, but now she felt a little tug in her chest. Was she really going to let a toy decide how happy she was?

She picked up Fluffy and hugged him. His fur was worn in the exact spots her hands always held. She remembered building a "Fort of Gold" out of those "boring" blocks, and how she and Fluffy had pretended they were guarding treasure from dragons. She had laughed so hard her stomach hurt that day.

Her happiness hadn't come from a robot. It had come from her imagination.

Uncle Marcus watched her quietly. "Zara," he said, "it's okay to like new things. But if you think, 'I'll only be happy when I get that,' you're putting your joy far, far away from you."

Zara took a slow breath. The Glow-Bot suddenly felt less like a magic key and more like just… another toy.

She closed the catalog. “I think I have enough,” she said.

The wanting shrank from a roaring fire into a tiny candle she could blow out. “Enough” wasn’t several toys; it was a decision. When she decided she had had enough, she became rich right where she sat—on the floor, with her blocks, her rabbit, and her own bright mind.

💭 What the Stoics Would Say

Seneca, one of the richest Romans, wrote:

“It is not the man who has too little, but the man who craves more, who is poor.”

If you always stare at what you lack, you live in a storm of poverty. The moment you say, “This is plenty,” you’ve found the strongest anchor.

🧠 Stoic Superpower

- **The “Enough” Shield:** When you see a cool new thing, say, “That’s nice, but I have enough.”
- **Catalog Close:** If ads make you feel “less,” close the book or screen and look at what’s already in your hands.

- **The "Already Enough" List:** Each morning, name three things you have that help make your life easier or better.

🔍 Your Turn to Reflect

- Think of a toy you "had to have" last year. Do you play with it as much as you imagined?
- Why does the wanting feeling return soon after we get something new?
- If you could keep only three things from your room, which would you choose?

Chapter 34

The Hand-Me-Down Bike (Finding Value in Use, Not "Newness")

Kian's bike was forest green, with chipped paint, a little rip in the seat, and gray tape wrapped around the handlebars. It had once belonged to his cousin, and now it was his trusty ride. The bell gave a tired little *ding*, but it always worked. The tires were worn, but they gripped the sidewalk like they knew every crack by heart.

Most days, Kian didn't think about how his bike looked. He thought about where it could take him.

One Saturday, he rode to the park to meet his friends. As he rolled up, he heard a *BEEP-WOOO* that sounded like a robot trying to sing. His friend Jace zoomed into view on a shiny new metallic-red bike with lights on the spokes, silver pegs on the back wheel, and a siren horn on the handlebars.

"Check this out!" Jace said, spinning in a circle so the lights flashed. "It's the Turbo Blaster 3000. Just got it yesterday."

Kian looked at his own forest-green bike. The paint was scratched. The tape on the handlebars was peeling a little at the edges.

"Whoa," Jace said, eyeing it. "Your bike looks like it survived a dinosaur attack. When are you getting a real one?"

Kian felt his cheeks get hot. He hadn't minded the scratches before, but now they felt like giant neon signs. Suddenly, his old bike didn't seem cool at all.

Grandpa, who had come along and was tightening the chain on Kian's bike, heard every word. He clicked the chain into place and wiped his hands on a rag.

"Well now," Grandpa said, "Jace's bike is very pretty. Looks like it belongs in a store window."

"But it's fast!" Kian said, a little defensively.

"Hmm," Grandpa said. "Let's find out."

They walked over to the dirt trail at the edge of the park. It twisted through trees, over roots, and around small rocks.

"First to the oak tree gets the biggest slice of pie tonight," Grandpa said with a grin.

Jace grinned back and took off like a rocket. His siren horn whooped as he sped ahead. Kian pushed down hard on his pedals and followed.

Halfway down the trail, a thick root stuck out across the path. Jace's shiny bike hit it with a *CRACK*. One of his plastic pedals snapped, and his foot slipped off.

"Hey!" Jace shouted, wobbling to a stop.

Kian's old bike bumped over the same root, rolled through the dirt, and kept right on going. It didn't mind a few bumps. It had seen worse.

He reached the oak tree first and skidded to a dusty stop. His heart pounded, but he was smiling.

Grandpa caught up, walking and clapping slowly. "See, Kian," he said, "new things can look fancy, but useful things are the real champs."

Jace limped his bike over, looking annoyed at the broken pedal. Kian glanced down at his own bike. The scratches didn't make it ugly. They made it special. They were proof of all the places it had taken him—races, errands, sunsets, and now one very important pie race.

He realized something: he didn't need the shiniest bike at the park. He needed a bike that could carry him where he wanted to go.

From that day on, when Kian saw his forest-green bike, he didn't see "old" or "hand-me-down." He saw a partner. He cared less about shine and more about where a bike could take him.

💭 What the Stoics Would Say

The Stoics taught that nature doesn't ask us to be fancy. If something does its job, it's enough.

If you have a bowl to eat from, a shirt for warmth, or a bike that rolls, you already have what you need. Gold paint doesn't make something better; it just makes it more expensive.

🧠 Stoic Superpower

- **Usefulness Test:** When you want something new, ask, "Does this do the job better than what I have?"
- **Scratches-Are-History Rule:** A scuffed ball or chipped bike means you're actually living, not running a museum.
- **Function Over Fashion:** Remind yourself: "This serves its purpose. That's what matters."

🔍 Your Turn to Reflect

- Is "new" always better? Is a new pen better than an old one if both write?
- Have you had a toy so "perfect" you were afraid to use it? How did that feel?
- Name one scuffed-up thing you've had the most fun with.

Chapter 35

The Quiet Saturday (Contentment, Without Needing a Screen)

Nico stared at his tablet. The screen was black. Completely, totally, stubbornly black.

He pressed the power button. Nothing. He wiggled the charger. The cord sparked once and then drooped like a tired noodle.

"It's dead," Mom said, testing it in another outlet. "The charger's broken. We'll have to get a new one on Monday."

Nico flopped onto the couch. "My Saturday is deleted," he groaned.

Boredom felt like a heavy, itchy blanket. Without games and videos, the living room seemed huge and empty. The clock ticked too loudly. The air felt too still.

His sister Elara sat by the window with a sketchbook, drawing slow, careful lines. "You look like you're waiting for the walls to entertain you," she said.

"There's nothing to do. It's too quiet," Nico muttered.

Elara raised an eyebrow. "The Stoics loved quiet," she said. "If you need a machine to be happy, you're its prisoner. If you can be happy with your brain and a piece of string, you're the boss.

You have an Inner Citadel—a fortress inside you that doesn't need Wi-Fi."

Nico frowned. "A fortress? Inside me?"

"Yep," Elara said. "It's the part of you that can make fun out of almost anything—if you let it."

Nico looked around. His first thought was, This room is boring. But then he really looked.

He saw his hands—ten fingers that could build, stack, throw, draw. He saw a pile of laundry with three lonely socks that had lost their partners. He saw a cardboard box by the trash can, waiting to be flattened. He watched the shadows from the window make shapes on the floor.

He took a deep breath and decided to run a little experiment: for one hour, he would stop being a consumer and start being a creator.

He grabbed the three mismatched socks and some rubber bands from the junk drawer. Could he juggle them? At first, they just flew in random directions and hit him on the head. He laughed and tried again. Slowly, he learned to toss one, then two, then three.

Next, he dragged the cardboard box into the middle of the room. Could he turn it into a goal? He crumpled scrap paper into balls and tried to kick them in from different distances. He made up points for trick shots: off the wall, off the couch, backwards.

The "desert" of the living room turned into an Olympic stadium. Nico wasn't scrolling; he was inventing. Between games, he noticed the sunlight crawling across the carpet, making warm patches. He heard the wind whoosh softly in the chimney and the tiny creaks of the house settling.

Without digital noise, he could hear something else: his own ideas.

By the time Mom checked on him, Nico was sweaty and smiling, with sock balls and paper scattered everywhere.

"What's all this?" she asked.

"It's my new game," Nico said proudly. "It's called Socks-Ball. I wrote the rules." He held up a paper with messy handwriting and little doodles.

Mom smiled. "Looks like your Saturday wasn't deleted after all."

Nico realized something important. The tablet hadn't been giving him fun; it had been hiding the fun he could create.

His Inner Citadel had been there the whole time—just waiting for a little quiet to wake up.

💭 What the Stoics Would Say

The Stoics believed that the need for constant entertainment weakens the mind. When you learn to enjoy quiet moments and simple things, your mind becomes stronger, braver, and more peaceful. A mind that can sit still, think, and notice small details is like a muscle that has been well-trained instead of one that always needs a toy to keep it busy.

🧠 Stoic Superpower

- **Boredom Bridge:** When you feel bored, wait five minutes before reaching for a screen. That's the bridge to new ideas.
- **Resourcefulness Challenge:** Pick one object (a spoon, rock, towel) and think of five ways to play with it.
- **Silence Scan:** Sit quietly and notice three sounds you usually ignore.

🔍 Your Turn to Reflect

- When was your last screen-free day? What did you discover about your mind?
- Why does boredom feel hard at first but then turn creative?
- On a long car ride with no devices, how could you use your Inner Citadel?

Chapter 36

The View from Above (Realizing How Small Our "Big" Problems Really Are)

Kiran was having a Giant Problem day.

In the morning, he had tripped in the cafeteria and spilled his milk all over the floor. His tray clattered, everyone turned, and someone even clapped as a joke. His cheeks burned for an hour.

In the afternoon, he got a C on a spelling test he'd actually studied for. He had written "disaster" as "dissaster" and "important" as "importent." Red marks jumped out at him like angry little ants.

By evening, Kiran was sure the universe was against him.

"Everything is a disaster," he sighed, slumping onto the balcony. "Everyone saw me fall. My grades are ruined. My life is falling apart."

His cousin Anjali was already out there, lying on a blanket and peering through a pair of old binoculars at the sky.

"Come see," she said, sitting up and handing them to him.

Kiran pressed the binoculars to his eyes. At first he saw a blur. Then he focused on a tiny bright dot.

"That's Jupiter," Anjali said. "It's so big that about thirteen hundred Earths could fit inside it. And there's a storm there that's been spinning for hundreds of years."

Kiran blinked. From here, Jupiter looked peaceful and small. Just a speck of light.

"Now imagine you're standing on Jupiter, looking back," Anjali said. "Can you see our house?"

"No," Kiran laughed. "Earth is a speck."

"Can you see our school? The cafeteria floor? Your spilled milk?"

Kiran shook his head. "Not a chance."

He took a slow breath. Zoomed in, his problems were monsters—huge and loud and embarrassing. Zoomed out to the stars, they were grains of sand.

"The Stoics called this the View from Above," Anjali said. "It doesn't erase your feelings; it just reminds you that your life is part of a huge, beautiful universe. Your C on one spelling test doesn't change the stars."

Kiran looked up with his own eyes now. The sky stretched and stretched, full of tiny lights and endless dark. Somewhere in all that space was their small blue planet. On that planet was their city, then their street, then their building, then their balcony.

And on that balcony was Kiran, feeling like the center of everything—when really, he was one small, important piece of a much bigger picture.

The storm in his head began to shrink. In the big picture, he was still healthy, loved, and alive. Tomorrow, he could clean up another spill. He could study a little more. The universe was not against him; it was simply very, very big.

His giant problems were tiny ripples.

He felt as if he'd put down a heavy backpack he didn't realize he'd been carrying.

💭 What the Stoics Would Say

Marcus Aurelius wrote about looking at the stars and remembering the bigger picture.

When you feel stuck in embarrassment, annoyance, or worry, look up. The vastness of the universe can help remind you that this moment is small—and it will pass.

🧠 Stoic Superpower

- **Zoom-Out Tool:** When overwhelmed, imagine rising above your house, city, and then Earth. Look at your problem from space.

- **Star Perspective:** Tell one star your biggest worry and remember it has seen billions of worries come and go.
- **Map Mindset:** Say, "I am one person in one house on one planet. My problem is one tiny dot."

🔍 Your Turn to Reflect

- Think of a "giant problem" from last year. How big does it feel now?
- Why do oceans or mountains often make us feel peaceful?
- As an astronaut, what big things on Earth would you notice instead of small ones?

Chapter 37

The Garden of Patience (Waiting for Things to Grow in Their Own Time)

Lila was a "Now" person. If she wanted to hear a song, she wanted it to start this second. If she wanted to learn a cartwheel, she wanted to be perfect by tomorrow. Waiting felt like a broken pause button on life.

For a school science project, her class was growing plants. Lila chose a sunflower. She liked the idea of something tall and bright that followed the sun.

She carefully pushed the seed into the soil of a little pot. She patted the top of the dirt and gave it a gentle drink of water.

Then she did what she always did.

She waited… for about five minutes.

She stared at the pot. Brown. Still. Quiet.

"Come on," Lila whispered. "Grow already."

Five minutes: nothing.

Ten minutes: still dirt.

Fifteen minutes: a stubborn, silent lump of soil.

"It's broken," she huffed, dropping the watering can. "I did everything right. I'm a bad gardener. This is a waste of time."

Her grandfather, who had a whole backyard full of tomatoes and herbs, sat down beside her.

"You're yelling at a mountain to move faster," he said gently. "Mountains and seeds don't have ears."

"But I'm waiting," Lila said. "And waiting is boring."

"Waiting only feels boring if you think you're losing time," Grandpa said. "The Stoics knew everything has its season. You can't force sunrise at midnight, and you can't force a flower in a minute. Patience isn't just waiting; it's staying calm while the world does its work."

"So I'm stuck?" she asked.

"No," he smiled. "You're in the Gap. While the seed grows roots where you can't see, you can grow your patience roots. Some of the best things are slow magic. Digging it up kills the magic."

Lila looked at the pot again. Her frustration wasn't helping the seed; it was only hurting her.

She took a long breath. "Okay, seed," she said quietly. "You do your part. I'll do mine."

Each day, she watered the pot without complaining. While she waited, she read stories on the porch, helped Grandpa pull weeds, and counted how many kinds of bugs she could spot.

When she stopped fighting the clock, boredom turned into quiet peace.

One morning, she went outside and froze. A tiny green speck poked through the soil, like a little fist saying hello.

Lila didn't scream or demand more. She just smiled.

The flower would grow tall and bright in its own time. But the patience she had grown inside herself—that invisible root system—felt even stronger.

💭 What the Stoics Would Say

Epictetus said:

"Nothing great comes into being all at once; not even the grape or the fig… If you tell me you want a fig, I answer that there must be time."

He was reminding his students that even simple things in nature need many quiet steps before they're ready: first a tiny bud, then a flower, then a small hard fruit, and only later something sweet you can finally eat. It's the same with you. From fruit to skills, everything needs a season. Muscles, music, friendships, confidence, and even calmness grow slowly, one practice, one choice, one small effort at a time.

🧠 Stoic Superpower

- **Slow Magic Mantra:** In long lines or waits, say, "This is slow magic; my roots are growing."
- **Not-My-Department Rule:** You control planting and watering; time belongs to the universe.
- **Waiting-Room Win:** Keep a go-to waiting activity—breath counting, room-observing, or gratitude listing.

🔍 Your Turn to Reflect

- What's something that took a long time but was worth it?
- Why doesn't "yelling at the dirt" speed anything up?
- How could you turn one boring wait tomorrow into root-growing time?

Chapter 38

The Shared Treat (Joy of Being a "Social Being")

Silas had saved for weeks for a Mega-Swirl sundae—the biggest one at the shop. It had three kinds of ice cream, hot fudge, sprinkles, and a cherry so bright it looked like it had its own spotlight. He had pictured it in his mind every day: him in the corner booth, headphones on, spoon in hand, eating every bite alone.

Today was finally Mega-Swirl day.

He jogged toward the shop, one hand on his five-dollar bill, already tasting the first cold, chocolatey bite in his imagination.

Outside the shop, he saw his friend Mateo sitting on the curb. Mateo's knees were scraped, his eyes shiny, and his soccer ball lay next to him, completely flat.

"I popped my ball and lost my snack money trying to fix it," Mateo sighed. "Not a good day."

Silas stopped. He could almost feel the cool air of the shop and smell the waffle cones. He glanced at the Mega-Swirl sign in the window: a mountain of ice cream, dripping fudge, perfect cherry on top.

He looked down at his five-dollar bill.

His Internal Audience was watching. He could choose the solo path or the social path. One path led to a giant sundae for one. The other led to something smaller on the table, but maybe bigger in his heart.

He remembered that the Stoics said humans are social beings—parts of one big human family. When one ship is sinking, other captains help patch the holes instead of sailing past.

Silas took a slow breath. The taste of fudge would last a few minutes; helping a friend might last all afternoon in his memory.

"I have enough for two small swirls," he said. "No giant cherry, but the fudge is the same. Want to join me?"

Mateo's head snapped up. "Really?" he asked.

"Really," Silas nodded.

They went inside and ordered two small swirls with hot fudge. No mountain of ice cream, no poster-worthy cherry, just two simple sundaes.

As they sat in the booth, Mateo told the whole story of the popped ball, and Silas told him about how long he'd been saving. They took turns stealing tiny spoonfuls of each other's toppings and laughing at the sticky mess on their hands.

Silas discovered a secret: joy doubles when you divide it. The smaller sundae tasted better because he wasn't just eating; he was connecting. His stomach felt full, but his chest felt even fuller.

💭 What the Stoics Would Say

Hierocles, a Stoic teacher, asked people to imagine themselves standing in the middle of many circles.

The smallest circle is you, then your family, then your friends and classmates, then your city, and finally all people everywhere.

He said a wise person gently "pulls the circles closer" by caring not only about themselves, but also about the people in the next circles. When Silas chose to share his sundae with Mateo, he was tugging that "friend circle" closer to his heart and acting like a true social being.

🧠 Stoic Superpower

- **Beehive Mindset:** When you have something good, ask, "Can I share a piece of this?"
- **Cooperation Check:** Tell yourself, "I'm part of a whole—my family, class, and world."
- **Double-Joy Rule:** When you're bored or sad, do something kind for someone else. caring for others is also good for you.

🔍 Your Turn to Reflect

- When has someone shared with you on a bad day? How did it change your "weather"?
- Why do we sometimes grab everything for ourselves?
- What small treat (snack, toy, time) could you share tomorrow?

Chapter 39

The Old Dog's Lesson (Living Fully in the "Now")

Pam walked her dog, Rufus, but her mind wasn't in the park. It was stuck in yesterday and tomorrow at the same time, like a movie with two different scenes playing on top of each other. Yesterday's history mistake replayed in her head on a loop, and tomorrow's swim meet loomed in front of her like a dark wave she wasn't sure she could surf.

She barely noticed where her feet were going. She missed the sharp, clean smell of pine needles, the sparkle of sunlight dancing on the pond, and the tiny concentric rings a duck made as it landed on the water. Her body was in the park, but her mind was time-traveling through regret and worry. She was a Captain who had left the wheel, letting her ship drift while she argued with yesterday and tried to control tomorrow.

Rufus, twelve years old with a gray muzzle and slow hips, was not time-traveling. He was fully here. He sniffed every bush like it was the most important smell in the world. He paused to feel the wind ruffle his ears. He wagged wildly when he discovered a muddy, half-chewed tennis ball, as if he'd found buried treasure.

"Rufus, you're old and slow," Pam said, half-teasing. "How are you so happy?"

She watched him for a moment longer and realized Rufus was a master of **Now**. He wasn't thinking about bones from years ago, or the vet visit on the calendar next month. The sun was warm now. Grass smelled green now. The ball was fun now.

Pam took a breath and looked down at her shoes. She decided, like a real Captain, to drop her anchor into this exact moment. She noticed the leash in her hand, rough against her fingers. She heard the crunch of gravel under her sneakers and the distant bark of another dog. She felt the air on her cheeks. The park seemed to brighten and sharpen, as if someone had adjusted the focus on a camera.

By worrying about tomorrow, she realized she had been quietly stealing joy from today. All that fear about the swim meet hadn't helped her swim a single stroke—it had only made this beautiful walk feel gray. She knelt and hugged Rufus, burying her face in his fur.

"Thanks for the lesson," she whispered. "Now is pretty great."

They walked on. This time, Pam kept gently bringing her mind back whenever it tried to time-travel. She spent the rest of the walk being exactly where her feet were.

💭 What the Stoics Would Say

Marcus Aurelius wrote:

"Remind yourself that it is not the future or the past that weighs on you, but always the present."

The past is gone, and the future isn't here yet—it exists only in your imagination. You can't carry tomorrow's problems today, because they don't exist as anything but thoughts. When you let go of yesterday, stop arguing with tomorrow, and come back to now, life feels lighter and more peaceful in the only time you can actually live: this moment.

🧠 Stoic Superpower

- **Feet Check:** When your mind time-travels, look at your feet and say, "My mind is where my feet are."
- **Five-Sense Feast:** Notice one thing you can see, hear, smell, feel, and taste right now.
- **Only-One-Day Rule:** Tell yourself, "I don't have to handle the whole week—just right now."

🔍 Your Turn to Reflect

- Do pets seem to worry about yesterday or tomorrow? What can you learn from them?
- Why does mind time-travel usually make us tired or stressed?
- What beautiful thing is happening right now that you might miss if you think only about tomorrow?

Chapter 40

The Sunset Reflection (Ending the Day with a Grateful Heart)

The sun was sinking, painting the sky violet and gold, like someone had tipped a giant watercolor brush over the edge of the world. Inside, Matt was in bed, the covers pulled up to his chest, but his mind was still zipping around like a firefly that wouldn't land.

He replayed the tower of blocks he had worked so hard on, crashing to the floor. He replayed his sister's teasing voice at dinner and the cookie he didn't get because there was only one left. Each memory felt like a little wave bumping his small ship, keeping it tossing long after the real storm was over.

Dad knocked softly and came in, sitting on the edge of the bed. "Time for the Sunset Scan?" he asked.

"The what?" Matt yawned, rubbing his eyes.

"The Stoics liked to sit on their mental mountain before sleep," Dad said. "They would look back over the day from above. Three quick questions—then you drop your anchor for the night."

Matt scooted up against his pillow. "What questions?"

"First: What did I do well today?" Dad asked.

Matt thought for a moment. "I helped Phil with math," he said slowly. "And I shared my markers at art time, even the good ones."

Dad nodded. "That's you noticing your wins, not just your wobble moments."

"Second," Dad continued, "where did I trip up—not to punish yourself, just to find the data."

Matt frowned a little. "I got really mad when I dropped my backpack," he said. "I yelled at Mom. I forgot my Stoic Gap and just exploded."

"That's okay," Dad said gently. "Now you know where to steer better tomorrow. That's what the Stoics did—turn mistakes into maps."

He held up three fingers. "Third: What am I grateful for right now?"

Matt looked around his room. "My bed," he said. "The way the sun looked like an orange falling into the trees. My stuffed turtle. You sitting here."

As he answered, the waves in his chest settled. The day's storm started to quiet, like the wind was finally calming down. He wasn't dragging the whole day into tomorrow; he was filing it away in neat little folders: Things I Did Well, Things I Can Improve, Things I'm Thankful For.

His shoulders relaxed into the pillow. The sunset wasn't just outside the window anymore; it was in his chest, a soft glow of peace and gratitude. His ship was no longer fighting the sea—it was resting in a calm harbor, anchor down, sails loose.

Matt's eyes grew heavy. As he drifted to sleep, he felt like a Captain who had checked his maps, cared for his crew, and was ready for a fresh voyage in the morning.

💭 What the Stoics Would Say

Seneca described this habit:

"When the light has been removed… I examine my entire day and go back over what I've done and said, hiding nothing from myself."

When you honestly review your day, you stop being pushed around by feelings and become the master of your character. Ending with gratitude cleans your ship for tomorrow.

🧠 Stoic Superpower

- **3-Question Scan:** Before sleep, ask: 1) What was a win? 2) What was a lesson? 3) What am I grateful for?
- **Mistake Eraser:** After learning from a mistake, imagine erasing it from a chalkboard. Don't carry it into tomorrow.

- **Gratitude Anchor:** Choose one small beautiful thing from the day and hold it in mind as you fall asleep.

🔍 Your Turn to Reflect

- If you did a Sunset Scan right now, what's one win from today?
- What's one lesson you learned from a mistake?
- Name three things you can feel or hear right now that you're grateful for.

Part 5: The Compass (Living Your Stoic Superpowers)

The Epilogue: Moving from reading stories to living a "Stoic Life" every single day.

A compass is only useful if you actually look at it while you hike. Stoicism is the same. It isn't just a book of stories; it's a way of breathing, thinking, and acting from the moment you wake up until the moment you close your eyes. This final part is about carrying your Stoic **Compass** in your pocket and actually using it.

Chapter 41

The Morning Mental Armor (Setting Your Intention Before the Day Starts)

Avery used to wake up like a leaf in a windstorm.

The moment her alarm went off, worry rushed in. Is it gym day? Did I finish my homework? What if the bus is late? What if I mess up reading aloud? Her thoughts spun faster than her ceiling fan. By the time she tied her shoes, her storm was already at Category 5. She was letting the day happen to her instead of deciding how she would meet the day.

One morning at practice, her coach noticed her tired eyes and tight shoulders.

"You look like you've already run three races," Coach said.

"I'm just thinking about everything that might go wrong," Avery admitted.

Coach gave her a new tool: mental armor. "Before you leave your room," Coach said, "you suit up. You wouldn't walk into a rainstorm without a coat. Don't walk into a feeling-storm without your Stoic armor."

So the next morning, Avery tried something new. She sat on the edge of her bed for two minutes. No phone. No rushing. Just her Morning Prep, like a quiet meeting with herself.

First, she would **expect the bumps**: "Today I'll probably meet someone grumpy. I might make a mistake. The bus might be crowded. Things might not go my way." Saying it out loud made the surprises feel less surprising.

Second, she would **choose the response**: "When that happens, I'll stay behind my Stoic shield. I'll breathe, use my Gap, and steer my own calm instead of letting other people steer me."

Third, she would **set the goal**: "My goal today isn't to be perfect; it's to be kind and brave. If I do that, today is a win."

Avery took a deep breath. She didn't feel magically fearless, but she felt steadier—like a tree with stronger roots.

On the way to the bus stop, a car splashed through a puddle, sending muddy water right onto her sneakers and the hem of her jeans. Normally, that would have lit a fire of anger and maybe even tears.

Avery felt the annoyance shoot up—and then felt her armor. I expected bumps, she thought. Wet shoes are just data. They're uncomfortable, but they don't change who I am or how I choose to act.

She shook off her feet, smiled a little at the squelching sound, and kept walking.

By preparing for the storm before it arrived, Avery had turned herself into something solid. She realized the morning isn't just for breakfast; it's for feeding your mind its plan and your heart the courage it needs for the day.

💭 What the Stoics Would Say

Marcus Aurelius wrote to himself every morning:

"When you wake up in the morning, tell yourself: The people I deal with today will be meddling, ungrateful, arrogant, dishonest, jealous, and surly... But I have seen the beauty of good, and the ugliness of evil, and I know that none of them can truly hurt me."

He didn't mean people are always bad; he meant we should **expect** difficult behavior. When you're not surprised by trouble, you don't lose your calm when it shows up.

🧠 Stoic Superpower

- **Two-Minute Prep:** Before you get out of bed, name one challenge you might face and one virtue (Patience, Courage, Justice, or Wisdom) you'll use.
- **Invisible Shield:** Imagine a glowing shield around you. Words and storms from others can hit it, but they don't get into your heart.
- **"I Am" Intention:** Finish: "Today, no matter what happens, I will be ______." (Helpful, steady, fair, etc.)

🔍 Your Turn to Reflect

- Do you usually start your day rushed or calm? How does that change how you handle the first mistake?
- Why does expecting problems make them feel smaller when they happen?
- What piece of armor do you want to "wear" tomorrow—Shield of Patience, Boots of Courage, or something else?

Chapter 42

The Evening Review (The Coach's Secret)

Emery had a mixed-bag day.

She helped a friend find a lost earring at recess (a win), but she also snapped at her brother when he touched her Lego tower (a trip-up). She spilled some juice at lunch, aced a spelling word she'd been practicing, and forgot to say thank you when her mom brought her favorite snack. It was one of those days that felt a little bit good, a little bit bad, and a lot confusing.

Usually, she would just fall into bed, pull the covers over her head, and hope tomorrow would somehow be better on its own. But a Stoic doesn't let the day vanish; they use it.

Before turning out the lamp, Emery opened her small notebook—her Captain's Log. It didn't have glitter pens or long, fancy paragraphs. She wasn't writing a big diary. She was doing a quick Evening Review, like a coach watching game footage after the players go home.

"Okay," she whispered. "Review time."

First came **Playback**. She closed her eyes and watched the "movie" of her day from morning to night. She saw herself yelling at her brother, saw his surprised face, and heard her own sharp voice. Instead of saying, "I'm a bad sister," she stayed in the Gap and asked, "What lit that fire?" She noticed she'd been tired, hungry, and worried about homework all at once. The snapping wasn't random—it had reasons.

Next came **Correction**. Emery didn't just feel sorry and stop there; she made a tiny plan. She wrote, "Next time I'm hungry and annoyed, I'll breathe before speaking and tell my brother I need five quiet minutes." That way, her mistake wasn't just a sad memory—it became a practice drill for tomorrow.

Then came **Success**. She remembered the lost earring and how her friend's face lit up with relief. She remembered holding the spelling test with the word she'd gotten right. She felt the solid glow of having helped someone and having tried hard. She told herself, "That felt right. Do more of that."

Emery was turning the mess of the day into lessons. A mistake wasn't a failure; it was a map for tomorrow. A good moment wasn't an accident; it was a move she could repeat on purpose.

When she pulled up the covers, she didn't just feel grateful; she felt prepared. She had checked her compass, marked her rough spots, circled her bright spots, and gently adjusted her course for the next day.

A coach's secret was now hers: review the game, learn, and rest ready.

💭 What the Stoics Would Say

Seneca loved this practice. He wrote:

"How good is this habit of examining the whole day! How calm is the sleep which follows… when the soul has either praised or admonished itself."

By praising your good actions and correcting your weak spots, you clear your conscience. You don't lie awake worrying about who you are—you know you're working on who you're becoming.

🧠 Stoic Superpower

- **Game-Film Technique:** Imagine your day as a game replay. Where were you the hero? Where did you foul? How can you change that play tomorrow?
- **No-Blame Rule:** Don't call yourself names. A scientist doesn't yell at a bubbling test tube; they adjust the formula. Adjust your "formula" for tomorrow.
- **One-Sentence Log:** Keep a notebook by your bed. Write one thing you want to do a bit better tomorrow.

🔍 Your Turn to Reflect

- If you were a coach watching your day, what's one "play" you'd run again?
- What's one play you'd change, and how?
- Why does honestly admitting a mistake feel better than hiding it?

Chapter 43

The Stoic Friend (The Lighthouse in the Storm)

The fifth-grade hallway felt like a Category 5 storm.

The field trip to Adventure Park had just been canceled because the bus engine failed. Kids slumped against lockers like umbrellas turned inside out. Some shouted about how unfair life was. One boy kicked his backpack in a full-on fire of anger. Another announced loudly, “School is the worst place on Earth!”

Felix felt the pull, like a strong wind tugging at his jacket. He wanted to complain too, to stomp and say, “Why does this always happen to us?” But he remembered his Compass—those Stoic ideas he'd been practicing.

He took a slow breath. He couldn't fix the bus or the school's decision—those were out of his control. But he could choose the weather he brought to the hallway.

He walked over and sat near his friend Sam, who looked close to tears, jacket hood half over his face.

“It really stinks, doesn't it?” Felix said.

He didn't say “Stop crying” or “It's not a big deal.” A Stoic friend is kind, not cold. They don't pretend the rain is sunshine; they just hold the umbrella with you.

"It's the worst day ever," Sam groaned. "Everything is ruined."

Felix thought for a moment. "The trip is ruined," he agreed. "That part is true. But is the day ruined? We still have lunch, and Mr. Henderson said we can have a board-game tournament in the gym. Not Adventure Park—but still an adventure."

Sam sniffed. "It won't be the same."

"Yeah," Felix said. "It won't. But maybe it can still be good in a different way."

Felix didn't preach. He didn't give a speech about fate or say, "You should just be positive." He just sat down, pulled out a deck of cards from his backpack, and started shuffling on the floor, the soft slap-slap-slap of the cards cutting through the noise.

One by one, kids stopped shouting and glanced over. Felix wasn't panicked or furious. He was steady, like a lighthouse on the shore while the waves crashed.

"Can I play?" someone asked, sliding down the wall.

"Sure," Felix said, dealing a card.

Then another kid asked. And another. Ten minutes later, the hallway had turned from Disaster Zone into Game Zone. There were still some grumbles, but now there was also laughter, teasing, and the clack of game pieces on the floor.

Felix hadn't forced anyone to cheer up, and he hadn't fixed the broken bus. But by being a lighthouse—a calm, kind friend—

he gave everyone something solid to steer toward when their feelings were stormy.

💭 What the Stoics Would Say

Epictetus wrote:

"When you see someone weeping in grief... do not be hurried away by the appearance... show him sympathy in words, but take care that you do not also lament internally."

You can be a great friend by listening and caring, without letting their storm sink your ship. Your calm is like a lighthouse that gives them something steady to steer toward until their storm passes.

🧠 Stoic Superpower

- **Lighthouse Effect:** When everyone is complaining, be the one who says, "Okay—what's our next move?" Calm is contagious.
- **"I Hear You" Tool:** You don't have to say "It's not a big deal." Just say, "I hear you. That's tough," and stay steady.
- **Calm Action:** Don't *tell* others to calm down. *Show* it—start a game, open a book, or just breathe slowly.

🔍 Your Turn to Reflect

- Who in your life stays calm when things go wrong? How does it feel to be around them?
- Why is it harder to stay calm when everyone else is upset?
- Next time a friend has a storm, how can you be a lighthouse without turning into a lecturer?

Chapter 44

The Never-Ending Journey (Stoicism Is a Practice, not a destination)

All the kids you've met—Leo, Sofia, Chloe, Toby, Ben, Zoe, Oliver, Ethan, Lucas, Sienna, Maya, Clara, Mason, Ava, Finn, Sam, and more—went back to their lives. None of them became perfect. They still got mad, scared, jealous, or sad. They still spilled things, argued, got grades they didn't like, and forgot their Stoic tools sometimes. The difference was simple: they now had a Compass.

One Tuesday, Theo was fixing his bike when a bolt snapped. For a second, the fire flared. He wanted to throw the wrench and shout that life was unfair. He almost lost his Gap. His face got hot, his fists tightened—and then he remembered.

He stopped and breathed. "I almost lost it there," he said to himself. He didn't think. I read 44 stories, and I'm still angry—what's wrong with me? He smiled instead.

Stoicism isn't a finish line; it's a practice. Being a Stoic is like being a musician or an athlete. You don't learn it once and quit. You practice. Some days you hit the right notes. Some days you miss. The important part is picking up the instrument again.

Theo picked up the wrench. The broken bolt was just data. He went to find a new one and tried again. That small choice—

catching himself, adjusting, and moving forward—was Stoicism in real life.

As the sun set on our 44 stories, each kid realized the same thing: the Mountain of character is tall, and the climb never really ends—and that's good news. There will always be new storms to steer through, new walls to turn into paths, and new small joys to notice if you're paying attention.

They weren't just reading a book anymore. They were living a life. They were Captains of their own choices, builders of their own Inner Citadel, and keepers of their own calm. Sometimes they would forget and hand the wheel to anger or fear—but now they knew how to take it back.

As long as they kept their Compass in hand and their breath steady, they were ready for whatever the great ocean of life brought next. And so are you. Every morning is a new chance to practice, and every small choice is another step up your Mountain.

💭 What the Stoics Would Say

Epictetus warned his students not to brag about being 'philosophers' but to live it. He said:

"Sheep do not bring back the grass to show the shepherds how much they have eaten; but, inwardly digesting their food, they outwardly produce wool and milk."

Don't just talk about being a Stoic or tell people you read this book. Digest it. Show your Stoicism in your **actions**—in kindness, honesty, and calm when things are hard.

🧠 Stoic Superpower

- **"Day One" Mindset:** Every morning is Day One. Yesterday's grumpiness doesn't stop you from being a Mountain today.
- **Practice Habit:** Remember: "Stoic" is a verb. It's something you *do*, not just something you call yourself.
- **Compass Check:** Whenever you feel lost, ask: "Is this in my control? What is the data? Am I acting like a good social being?"

🔍 Your Turn to Reflect

- Which story in this book is your favorite? Why did it stick with you?
- Which Stoic tool (Gap, Anchor, View from Above, Compass, etc.) do you think you'll use most this week?
- If you wrote a Chapter 45 about your own life, what would the title be?

The Epilogue

Your Stoic Life

You've reached the end of the book, but you're only at the beginning of your adventure. You now have a chest full of tools and a fortress in your mind that no one can take away.

The world will still be loud. Rain will still fall on picnic days. People will still be grumpy sometimes. But you? You are a Stoic kid. You know the sun is always behind the clouds, and the Mountain is always under your feet.

Keep climbing, Captain.

Request for a Review

Thank you so much for reading **Stoic Kids: Big Feelings Edition – 44 Stories to Help Kids Handle Anger, Anxiety, and Self-Control**.

I hope these stories inspired calmness, courage, kindness, and thoughtful reflection—for both you and the young reader in your life.

If this book made a positive difference in your home, classroom, or heart, I'd be truly grateful if you could take a moment to leave a review. Your feedback helps other readers discover this book and allows me to keep creating meaningful content for young minds. Even a sentence or two can make a big impact.

You can leave a review here:

Thank you again for supporting thoughtful, character-building stories for kids. May your journey with Stoicism continue—one calm, kind, and courageous step at a time.

With gratitude,
Rodolfo

About the Author

Rodolfo Costa is a lifelong learner with a deep passion for Stoic philosophy and personal growth. His books—including *The Stoic Path*, *The Stoic Prompt Journal*, *The Calm Within*, and *Advice My Parents Gave Me*—have inspired readers of all ages to live with more wisdom, calm, and courage.

With a background in business, real estate, and self-development, Rodolfo brings Stoic ideas to life in a way that is practical, relatable, and full of heart. With the **Stoic Kids** series, he is on a mission to help young readers discover the tools they already have inside them—like patience, kindness, honesty, and self-control.

He lives in Northern California, where he continues to study, write, and walk the Stoic path every day. Through his books, Rodolfo hopes to make philosophy not just something you read—but something you live.

www.ingramcontent.com/pod-product-compliance
Lightning Source LLC
LaVergne TN
LVHW020715110826
845149LV00012B/2275
* 9 7 9 8 9 9 3 6 2 7 0 1 4 *